THE COOPERATIVE PRINCIPLE OF FREEWAY DRIVING

FRED SPRUELL
AKA
FREDERICK RULE

Copyright © 2024 by Fred Spruell AKA Frederick Rule

ISBN: 978-1-77883-272-7 (Paperback)
        978-1-77883-273-4 (Hardback)

All rights reserved. No part of this publication may be reproduced, distributed, or transmitted in any form or by any means, including photocopying, recording, or other electronic or mechanical methods, without the prior written permission of the publisher, except in the case brief quotations embodied in critical reviews and other noncommercial uses permitted by copyright law.

The views expressed in this book are solely those of the author and do not necessarily reflect the views of the publisher, and the publisher hereby disclaims any responsibility for them.

BookSide Press
877-741-8091
www.booksidepress.com
orders@booksidepress.com

Fred Spruell
(aka Frederick Rule)
M.A. Candidate
Psychology
International College
Los Angeles, California

The Cooperative Principle of Freeway Driving
A thesis submitted in partial fulfillment
of the requirements for the degree of
M.A. in Psychology

Contents

Chapter 1: The Problem — 1
Introduction 1
Problem Statement 4
Background 4
Purpose 5
Significance 6
Methodology 7

Chapter II: Literature Review — 9
Introduction 9
Mechanistic Models of Driving: A System Without People 10
The Shortcomings of the Ramp Meter Solution 12
The Gore Point 13
The Summer Games Model of Freeway Efficiency ...15
The Solitary Driver Model: People Without a System 19
Expressive Driving 24
Driving as a Road Warrior 26
Toward an Interpretive Model of Driving:
A Critique of the Mechanistic and Behavioral Models 29
A Cooperative Model of Driving:
People Working in Systems 32
The Gestalt of Driving in a System 32
Freeway Driving as Culture 34

Chapter III: Design of the Study — 39
Introduction 39
Hypothesis 40
Definition of Terms 40

Assumptions..41
Scope and Limitations 41
Procedure 43
Data Gathering 43
Articulating the Cooperative Model: Theoretical Foundations ..44
The Cooperative Principle of Freeway Driving.......................45
The Consequences of Violating Cooperation 47
Testing the Cooperative Principle:
The Cooperative Model vs. the Behaviorist Model.................52
The Cooperative Principle and the Psycho-Social Model.........53
The Cooperative Model: Rules Over Laws 56
The Limits of Laws..57
The Implicature of BABY ON BOARD 61

Chapter IV: Results and Discussion   63
Results..63
Discussion...64

Chapter V: Recommendations   65
From Theory to Practice 65
Traffic Safety Campaigns 66
During a Typical 75-Years Lifespan You: 67
Effectiveness of 70% Safety Belt Usage 67
Traffic Violators' Schools 68
Therapy and Driving..72
The Viscott Method and Freeways...........................74
Long-Range Consequences.....................................75
The Cooperative Principle and the Synergistic Society............75

List of Resources   78

Abstract

This study investigates the power of a cooperative model to explain the traffic psychology of the freeway. In contrast to dominant models of traffic analysis, which either ignore the role of affect and interpretation in the driving task or ignore the fact that the freeway is a system with "specific field conditions" (Sporli 1978; cited in Bliersbach and Dellen 1980), the cooperative model concentrates on the psycho-social dimensions of the freeway system. Adopting the model of cooperative activity from the philosopher H.P. Grice, this thesis argues that two unconscious rules, or maxims, govern freeway driving—<u>Be safe</u> and <u>Be swift</u>—and that violating these maxims is the cause of competitiveness and frustration while driving.

When tested against these existing studies, the cooperative model can explain the limitations of existing traffic safety campaigns without the cooperative model, and the specific ways that freeway drivers can improve the efficiency of the freeway system and reduce their own stress.

Program Description:

Although this program is useful for any age it is designed for middle and high school teens. The <u>Cooperative Model</u> is a highly interactive team oriented driver education program where, the instructor plays the role of facilitator. The facilitator will use a variety of California driving resource's in conjunction with the cooperative principle, such as existing driving pamphlets, videos, and textbooks as well as simulators if available. This program will also use interactive video segments acted in and created by participants, small group discussions, role-play, short lectures and a **"chat room";** where participants can share stories, grievances and come up with new cooperative ideas.

The Cooperative Model will consist of 20 sessions; designed to encourage cooperation, which will help young drivers develop confidence and strategies that will allow them to be safe, informed and poised on the road. Teambuilding games and learning activities will be interjected in every session. This program will also encourage collaboration instead of retaliation when involved in traffic disputes. The hope is that cooperation will expand into other areas of their lives as well.

Long-term goals:

A cooperative model will reduce the number of injuries and fatalities, by creating better drivers and safer highway conditions. Additionally the cooperative model will reduce stress and congestions on the nation's highways. The goal of the cooperative model is to augment not replace existing models. However current traffic schools and driver education programs in Los Angeles will be discussed and analyzed and recommendations for a psycho-social component will be made.

The cooperative model asserts that a major cause of congestion on our freeway systems is largely due to a lack of cooperation amongst drivers. The cooperative models will take on an effort to revolutionize the traffic system in a way that will not only make it safer but will put pleasure back into the driving experience.

This program will carry forward studies into areas recommended by recent literature on traffic psychology. According to the existing literature, such a model is significantly lacking in existing programs:

In his article entitled "The Effects and Efficiency of Traffic Safety Campaigns," G.S. Wilde states, "It is beginning to be realized how important social factors are and how much of the behavior of people in traffic is influenced by that which they see in others." However, the history of studies on driving shows that until recently there has been virtually no interest in freeway driving as a social subsystem. Therefore, psycho-social models of driving, especially those that highlight the cooperative and interpretive nature of driving, are being called for by both traffic psychologist and traffic safety programs.

The cooperative model assumes:

1) That Freeway driving demands intense cooperation among participants.
2) That freeway interactions can be seen as a subsystem of social interactions in general.
3) That traffic safety campaigns and traffic schools depend for their strategy upon a theoretical model of traffic psychology.

4) That a personal understanding of the cooperative nature of freeway driving can be a crucial step toward safer and less stressful driving habits.

Length:
Two Semesters per school year

Class Size:
12 to 15 participants Maximum 20.

Language:
English, Spanish and a variety of other languages spoken in the Los Angeles area.

Introductions:
- Ice Breakers
- Get acquainted
- Expectations and guidelines

The Team Concept: Begs the question, are we as smart as a **goose?**

This spring when you see geese heading back north for the summer flying along in a **"V"** formation, you might be interested in knowing what scientists have discovered about why they fly that way. It has been learned that as each bird, flaps its wings, it creates uplift for the bird immediately following. By flying in a **"V"** formation, the whole flock adds at least 71% greater flying range than if each bird flew on its own.

Five Dysfunctions of a Team: Author Patrick Lencioni

- o   Absence of Trust
- o   Fear of conflict.
- o   Lack of commitment.
- o   Avoidance of Accountability.
- o   Inattention to Results.

What's Needed?
- Build Trust
- Conflict Norming
- Achieve Commitment
- Hold People Accountable
- Focus on Results

Create Teachable moment:
(Teambuilding Activities)
1. Trust Fall
2. Open Hand Versus Clinched Fist.
3. Helium Stick
4. The Mouse Trap
5. The Key Punch

Simulation:
- ☐ Replicate real-time freeway system and city streets as well as traffic problems and adverse conditions.
- ☐ Provide solutions to traffic problems in real-time using the cooperative model as a tool.

Teen second life:

- ✓ A virtual interactive world for teen to talk traffic.
- ✓ Share driving experiences with teens from other states, countries and cultures.

Does:

i. **Cautious mean safe?** No. (driving too cautious often creates confusion for other drivers)

ii. **Courteous mean cooperative?** No. (being overly courteous can create as much a danger as driving reckless)

iii. **Speed kill?** No. There are lots of factors that come in to play in fatal accidents speed is just one. Researchers indicate that variance in speed is much more of a factor i.e. variations between the slow cars and fast cars in the same space. From an excerpt written by Charles Lave in AAA Foundation For Traffic Safety. "Did the 65 MPH Speed Limit Save Lives"? "This study looks at the statewide consequences of raising the speed limit, treating highways and enforcement as a total system. Contrary to the conclusion of the local-effect studies, we find that the 65 mph speed limit reduced the statewide fatality rate by 3.4-5. 1 percent, compared to those states that did not raise their speed limits."

Core curriculum:

- Start an open-ended dialogue with teens on whether changing attitudes and behaviors can be the first's steps toward changing the world of driving.

- Construct a form of driving that will assist participants to remain aware and in the moment.
- Contrast defensive driving with a cooperative model.
- Explore "Micro motives Macro Behaviors".
- Critique the mechanistic and behavioral models

Experiential learning

- Take participants on field trip focus on cooperative driving.
- Shoot video of traffic on surface street as well as the freeway, compare to videos on existing models.
- When appropriate will video student's driving on surface streets and Freeways observe and have open dialogue.
- Have participants play the role of pedestrian as well as that of the driver i.e. both are central to the functioning of a cooperative system.

Real Time Learning:

Safe Moves:

Students will drive battery-operated cars (Golf Cars) through a secured area of the city designed to replicate a real time driving experience, "Safe Moves City" and are asked to perform basic driving skills. Through this exercise of maneuvering the car through the city streets, the student driver will experience twenty (20) potential collisions including a child running across the street mid-block, a teen crossing against the light or a bicyclist running a red light.

This experience will not only alert the students to the high level of skill needed to drive, but also allow them to experience their own vulnerability as a pedestrian, bicyclist and motor vehicle operator in traffic. By taking the role of the driver, students will see how easily they can be distracted and the importance of a high level of concentration needed to perform as a safe driver.

Why the Cooperative Model:

It is the only model that offers the best chances of reducing traffic accidents, traffic fatality, traffic congestions, reducing stress while driving and making the pedestrian an integral part of the traffic system.

Chapter 1

The Problem

Introduction

I begin with a story.

I am driving my four-by-four Bronco over Coldwater Canyon to the valley, and I come up behind a car going what I consider unusually slow. Because the road is very curvy and it is nearly impossible to pass, I feel trapped behind the slower driver. At first I am only slightly disappointed because I assume that the driver will pull over to let me pass at the next available turn out, which have been designed for that purpose. When that doesn't happen I begin to wonder.

Having expected cooperation but received none, I start to question the driver's intentions. Once I notice that the driver is an older woman, I begin to doubt her competence. Since I presume she does not understand my need, I pull up closer on her bumper, expecting her to get the message. When she does not pull over, I become angry and my thoughts about her become not only hostile but also stereotyped; she is an old woman, I think, an old white woman with blue hair.

The closer I get to her and the more I blow my horn, the slower she goes. And the slower she goes, the less powerful I feel, the less worthwhile, and the more frustrated. And the more frustrated, the more I want to punish her.

Suddenly I realize that she too might be getting emotional. Does she wonder whom the black man is driving a large jeep-like vehicle bearing down on her bumper on the dangerous mountain road? Does she think I have no concern for her safety? With these questions in my head, I pull back from her bumper and follow her slowly down the mountain.

By the time that we reach the bottom of the hill and I am able to pull beside her, I have come to understand that what has just occurred is not merely a driving incident but an interpersonal one. We have been communicating and miscommunicating for the last several miles. And because I faulted her as a driver, I have assigned all kinds of blame to her as a person. Having learned from this incident, I am no longer angry when I pull beside her. I am, in fact, thankful. So instead of a hostile gesture or an angry word, I look at her as sweetly and understandable as I can. When she returns my look, and shows obvious surprise that I am not hostile, I know that we have made contact—human contact.

There are several dimensions of this story that should interest psychologists. The first dimension is the affective quality of the interaction. Driving, as we all know, is a very affective task. Most drivers openly express feelings on the highway—feelings which range from anger and frustration to joy, relief, and gratitude. In fact, these feelings seem closer to the surface when driving than at any other time. This can partially be explained by the fact that driving is dangerous, and even though we might not be aware of it consciously, we unconsciously expect others to drive safely and efficiently to protect themselves as well as us. When there is evidence to the contrary, our life is endangered and our feelings are intensified. While this is only a partial explanation, the fact remains that people express feelings while driving, feelings that many times would be unacceptable to express in other circumstances.

The second important dimension of this story concerns the necessity of interpretation by drivers. Because there are no hard and fast rules or strict laws about mountain driving, such as who should pull over and when, I was forced to interpret the other driver's actions before I could decide how to act. Moreover, with each new interpretation, my feelings changed. At first I was angry at the woman's incompetence; then I was judgmental; finally, after reinterpreting the event from her perspective, I was able to relax and develop benevolent feelings. Only by constant reinterpretation of the meaning of their actions could I reach the point where I could express forgiveness, understanding, and love. Despite laws and safety guidelines, the driving test demands a great deal of constant interpretation.

The third and most significant aspect of this story, since it will comprise the focus of my thesis, is the cooperative. Since I was driving on a dangerously hilly mountain road, I expected cooperation from fellow drivers. When I did not receive it, I became upset. This breakdown in cooperation forced me into interpretation and inspired my emotional reactions. The significant result of the violation reveals how important the expectation of cooperation is while driving, not only on mountain roads but whenever one meets other drivers.

I extend the discussion of these rather obvious dimensions of the story to make a point. Even though a careful psycho-social analysis of this event brings out the crucial affective, interpretive, and cooperative features of driving, the vast majority of psychological models of the driving task either diminish the importance of these features or ignore them completely.

In his influential article "Social Interaction Patterns in Driver Behavior: An Introductory Review," traffic psychologist G.J.S.

Wilde (1976) states "It is beginning to be realized how important social factors are and how much of the behavior of people in traffic is influenced by what they see in others" (492). Although Wilde calls for a psychological study of driving that reminds drivers that they are not alone on the highway, there have been few studies since Wilde's article that explain the social factors of driving in any precise way. In fact, most scholars of the driving task show virtually no interest in seeing driving as a social subsystem. More significant is that traffic safety campaigns—such as public service announcements, driving schools or traffic violators' schools—also do not take into account the social dimensions of driving.

What is needed, therefore, is a psycho-social model of driving that explains what others have ignored: the affective, interpretive and most importantly, the <u>cooperative</u> nature of the driving experience. Developing that model and testing its explanatory power will be the goal of this thesis.

Problem Statement

Existing models of the psychology of driving ignore crucial social and interactive elements. How influential are these elements? A cooperative model of traffic psychology should tell us what these models cannot, and it should be able to help educate those who design safety programs so that our highways can be safer and more efficient.

Background

As Donald H. Taylor, traffic psychologist, points out, current models of the driving task are limited to ergonomic, or mechanistic, and the behavioral (Taylor 1980). The mechanistic model of driving treats traffic as a potentially efficient man-machine system, which is complicated only by untrained, inexperienced, or unrestrained drivers. Although this model explains a great deal about the engineering of the freeway system, its limitations become apparent when traffic safety campaigns follow this model. Trying to maintain the driving system though laws, traffic officers unfairly punish good drivers, who know that being safe and efficient sometimes means breaking the laws.

The second dominant model of driving is the behaviorist. This model, informed by behavioral psychology, is an improvement over the mechanistic one because it sees drivers as more than functions of an efficient system. Unfortunately, however, the behavioral model limits the psychological reality of driving to automatic reactions to stimuli: road signs, weather conditions, and other drivers become equally important stimuli. Such a model, says Taylor, ignores the social and interpretive nature of driving.

Taylor's argument is that these models of driving have two serious faults: 1) They do not explain many kinds of driving experiences (e.g., the story above), and 2) they do not adequately inform traffic safety efforts. In short, they neither make highways safer nor drivers more efficient. Thus, Taylor, among others, calls for an adequate psycho-social model of driving.

This thesis is a step toward that goal.

Purpose

The purpose of this thesis is to construct a psycho-social model of freeway driving that focuses on the affective, interpretive and cooperative elements of the activity. I will argue that existing accounts of the driving task are limited because they deny the human being behind the wheel, or deny that freeway driving is a system of interdependent actions and reactions. Contrary to dominant scholars in traffic psychology, my purpose is to produce safe and efficient drivers who are also healthy social beings.

Significance

If a cooperative model of traffic psychology can be formulated that explains a great deal of driving phenomena hitherto unexplained, that model should have significant influence on traffic safety campaigns, ultimately creating safer and more efficient freeway conditions and less stressful drivers.

The significance of such a consequence for the 700 miles of freeway system in the Los Angeles area alone cannot be underestimated. During a peak hour of freeway use, between 3000 and 5000 drivers are passing any particular point. And these drivers are constantly interacting with one another. Over 20,000 drivers must change lanes with one another during peak times at the Sherman Oaks junction to the San Diego Freeway (California D.M.V. 1984). The freeway—with all of its pleasures and frustrations—is part of the experience of millions of Los Angeles residents.

Yet because of congestion, the freeway driving experience for Los Angeles drivers is becoming increasingly frustrating. Currently over 200 miles (30%) of the Los Angeles freeway system operates at under 35 miles per hour during peak periods. And the amount of congestion is rapidly increasing, doubling in the last twenty years (Seale 1986). With this congestion comes an increasing number of Los Angeles drivers under stress, stress whose psychological toll upon personal and family health is only beginning to be studied.

Many therapists believe the traffic may be the single most stressful factor in Los Angeles life, more important than worries about crime or careers (Seale 1986:115). The reasons for this are easy to see. During the morning commute, for instance, drivers are under extreme social pressures; they are, in fact, acting out of a desire to survive. Thus, morning commuters are worried about survival whether the traffic is flowing or not. Not only must they hurry to work, since being late might jeopardize their economic survival, but when speeding along on the crowded freeway, they are physically endangered. At this speed one mistake could be fatal.

Not only does the stress of driving influence our general mental health, but there is also evidence that mental health may affect the way we drive—a phenomenon that should be of special interest to therapists. Dr. Ange Lobue, medical director of the Department of Psychiatry at Saint Francis Medical Center in Lynwood, has said, "For many people, the way they drive is an extension of the way they feel" (Seale 1986:111). As one Los Angeles writer puts it, "Like a 450-mile Rorschach inkblot test, the freeway ends up defining the parameters of our contemporary metropolitan souls" (Rufoff 1986).

Since the freeway experience is crucial to life in Los Angeles, and since that experience is becoming increasingly stressful and frustrating, my study, which allows us a clearer understanding of the interdependence between driving and social psychology, should be a significant step toward increasing the mental health of the entire city.

Methodology

The success of my thesis does not depend upon original empirical research. Rather, it depends upon developing a model of driving that successfully accounts for the existing data about driving behavior and that explains this data in more productive ways. Thus, my primary methodology will be to test the validity of the cooperative model against existing studies that dominate the discussion of freeway driving and which influence national and state policy.

Chapter II

Literature Review

Introduction

"Traffic, to many Los Angeles residents, seems much like the weather: everyone talks about it, but no one does anything" (Balter 1986:12). That statement, which appears in a quite sophisticated article about freeways in the Los Angeles Times Magazine, reveals how significant traffic is to people who live in Los Angeles. It is like the weather, something that surrounds our daily activities and affects our moods and activities. It is also, like some California weather, a catastrophe, a natural disaster that humans cannot control. Such is the perspective of many popular articles on the freeway, which usually express a naïve wonder about the freeway, about its danger when running smoothly and its frustration when congested. And it is no coincidence that two recent popular articles in Los Angeles magazines shared the title of Road Warriors (Balter 1986; Seale 1986), since both articles suggest that commuting now feels more like going to war than going to work.

At the same time that most popular articles about the freeway express either wonder or despair, several important scholarly studies have been written that try to account for the freeway phenomenon in precise terms. In this chapter, several representative studies of this type will be reviewed.

The organization of this chapter is dialectical. In section one, "Mechanistic Models of Driving: A System Without People," I will discuss the strengths and weaknesses of the "mechanistic" models of freeway driving developed by traffic engineers.

The next section, "The Solitary Driver Model: People Without a System," presents the standard psychological studies of the driving experience, focusing on the behaviorist and gestalt models.

The third major section, "Toward an Interpretive Model of Driving: A Critique of the Mechanistic and Behavioral Models of Driving," discusses the work of Donald H. Taylor, who discusses the limitations of the mechanistic and behavioral models.

The final section, "A Cooperative Model of Driving: People Working in Systems," reviews those studies that focus on the psycho-social, interactive, and cultural model of driving.

Mechanistic Models of Driving: A System Without People

The most influential arguments about what should be done to make freeways safer and more efficient come from traffic engineers. In California, these engineers work for the California Department of Transportation (Caltrans hereafter), which is responsible for highway design, roadway construction, and highway system maintenance, and most importantly, traffic management.

Traffic management, which involves the planning and management of commuter and event traffic, is considered by Caltrans to be a specialized field, requiring a precise knowledge of engineering. For example, traffic managers must determine how fast traffic is flowing on any freeway at any time. Within an instant they must tell if an incident has happened on the freeway and which lanes are blocked. In terms of state and local policy, traffic managers also must make recommendations about the feasibility of new freeway construction, recommendations whose scientific rigor are highly influential with government officials.

Yet the traffic engineering model of freeway driving has severe limitations. It views driving as merely a technical problem whose psychological and social dimensions can be ignored. As Bliersbach and Dellen (1980) describe it, in such a model, "The driver is seen as a neutral being whose rational interest in the proper functioning of traffic determines his own driving behavior" (475). Such an assumption—that the driver is not an important factor in creating an efficient driving system—is precisely the one that underlies the recommendations of Caltrans traffic engineers.

An archetypal example of the mechanistic approach can be found in the work of James D. Ortner, Ph. D and Principle Scientist of the Highway Engineering Department of the Automobile Club of Southern California. His paper, "Freeway Management," is written to challenge the "commonly held view" that freeway congestion is caused by a "failure to build needed freeway capacity." The truth is, he argues, that more freeways do not solve the problem; drivers merely congest them as quickly as they are built. What is needed instead, he says, is better management of existing freeways. And the key to managing existing freeways better lies in the increased use of freeway entrance ramp meters, which can control traffic flow at a smooth rate: "Metering rates must be set so that mainline freeway volumes are kept just below capacity and flow is smooth" (2).

Ortner's study was motivated by the evidence that "Despite the public perception that freeways get congested because they're carrying more vehicles, it is clear that peak hour vehicle volume actually drops." Ortner's evidence comes from automatic counting devices and cameras that measure the traffic flow around ramps with meters and those without.

Ortner's insights are important for several reasons: the first is, of course, their influence with government officials, who realize that funding for freeway construction is limited. Second, Ortner reminds us that freeways will not be a panacea; any strategies for change must =make the existing freeways more efficient, as my thesis tries to do. Finally, Ortner's discussion is significant because it reveals the essential shortcomings of the mechanistic model, shortcomings we shall review in some detail.

The Shortcomings of the Ramp Meter Solution

Attempts to solve freeway congestion through mechanistic suggestions like building more ramp meters are insufficient because they ignore crucial human factors. For example, Ortner's statistical method, which counts <u>vehicles</u> instead of <u>drivers</u> tends to treat all drivers as equal. The difference between these drivers, and the ways that they enter the traffic flow, is ignored. Ortner assumes that once drivers are released onto the accelerating lane they will merge smoothly and efficiently. That is, he assumes that every driver knows how to enter freeway traffic smoothly and can do so efficiently and without fear.

But that is not always the case. As a discussion of the <u>gore point</u> reveals, congestion may be caused not by <u>how many</u> drivers merge at one time but by <u>the way</u> that they merge.

The Gore Point

The gore point is that place on the freeway where the merging lane becomes part of the mainstream lane of traffic. The engineering principle of the gore point is that entering the flow of traffic at this point allows the driver to merge smoothly without causing the mainstream drivers to slow or brake. The most efficient way to do this is to reach the speed of the traffic flow and to merge at the gore point with only the slightest acceleration or deceleration.

While such a practice seems quite simple, it is not adopted by all drivers. There are a significant number of drivers who try to enter the traffic flow below the freeway speed or before they gore point. This practice causes other drivers to slow or brake and creates a domino effect: the driver who merges early and breaks the "barrier" usually cannot enter at the appropriate speed; other drivers must either brake or move to other lanes, which slows those lanes, which causes other drivers to brake, and so on.

The proposition, simply put, is that cars merging from the accelerating lane onto the freeway should use the full length of the lane before entering the traffic flow and should do so at the appropriate speed. Why don't more drivers follow the practice?

The primary reason for the inefficient use of the gore point cannot be explained by engineers, but it can be by a psychological approach. First of all, the gore point is not merely an abstract point on an engineer's graph; it is also a place where drivers must cooperate with one another. To be appropriate, the merging driver must wait until the gore point, and the mainstream driver must allow the driver to enter by either accelerating or decelerating slightly. The most efficient "weave effect" can only be created if both drivers are aware of their responsibilities at the precise moment when responsible action is needed. And this responsibility is not merely an act of efficiency; it is not merely an act that can be taught in traffic school. It is a social act. And thus only social reasons can explain why the gore point is not used effectively.

Entering the freeway at the gore point requires a great deal of trust. One must not only expect cooperation, one must depend on it. No matter how rational the proposition seems, or how effective it may be in reducing traffic congestion, merging at the gore point must be done without any assurance of cooperation from other drivers. It is a risky proposition. The driver must be willing to wait for the precise moment in which to act.

The inability to wait for this moment and merge efficiently has more to do with the driver's psychological state that traffic engineers realize. According to Dennis Munjack, a psychiatrist and director of the Anxiety Disorders clinic at USC, drivers who are fearful of the freeway manifest that fear by entering traffic timidly and slowly (Munjack 1986). Munjack's clinical evidence is also supported by Donna Dow, traffic helicopter announcer for KNX radio in Los Angeles, who observes, "We have a lot of drivers out there who are intimidated by the freeways. And you have volume builders and they can't get in and out of traffic quickly enough" (Dow 1986). And David Viscott provides an account of the psychological reasons for the inability to "get in and out of traffic quickly":

> Whatever your reasons for deciding to risk, if they are not arrived at by honest acceptance of yourself—who you are and where you are going—your risk becomes increasingly dangerous. You will be overwhelmed by your fears and dishonesty at the very point you must make a clear commitment (Viscott 1980:64).

The insights of Munjack, Dow, and Viscott reiterate the crucial human factors of driving that traffic engineers ignore, factors that often subvert the smooth running systems that they propose. As far as Ortner's recommendations are concerned, one might argue that since nearly 20,000 drivers (not vehicles) must enter the flow of traffic during peak hours at a typical interchange, it is likely that mental health of the drivers is just as important as the number of vehicles.

The Summer Games Model of Freeway Efficiency

David Roper, the Deputy Director of Caltrans, argues that the Los Angeles freeways could be made more efficient by adopting the traffic policies of the 1984 Olympics on a regular basis. Contrary to popular wisdom, Roper provides evidence that the efficiency of the freeways during the Olympics was not caused by fewer drivers. On the contrary, during that time, the freeways actually carried five percent <u>more</u> traffic than usual. The difference lay in the fact that this traffic was spread out during the day. Roper suggests that some of the traffic policies of that summer could create the same effect: "It would still work. The system is not outmoded. Now we are surging that system at the peak hour and destroying the efficiency of that system at a time when we most drastically need it." (Roper 1986).

Let us examine Roper's suggestions more closely. While Roper is correct in emphasizing that the freeway is a <u>system</u>, not merely a group of individual drivers, Roper's underlying model of freeway driving is, like Ortner's, a system without people. Like Ortner, and typical of mechanistic accounts, Roper assumes that all drivers are equally efficient; the only problem is how many there are.

And while it may seem logical to adopt the driving practices of the Olympics, those practices cannot be separated from the entire social context of the summer games. In reviewing recommendations like Roper's Jim Seale reminds us that many characteristics of the summer Olympics cannot be easily duplicated on a regular basis:

> These included the cancellation of all roadwork and the well-publicized fear of gridlock that kept some people off the freeways. There was also the fact that many companies went on staggered shifts, flextime or four-day work weeks—a practice that spread the traffic more evenly throughout the day… Another important variable in the congestion picture, truck traffic, was neutralized during the Olympics. Overall truck traffic was down only 10 percent, yet daytime truck volume was down 50 percent. It was the result of localities temporarily repealing ordinances that prohibit trucks from traveling and making deliveries at night, when most trucking companies would prefer to deliver (Foutz 1985).

As Seale's list demonstrates, the efficiency of the freeway during the Olympics was not merely the result of fewer or more well-spaced vehicles, as Roper implies. On the contrary, the freeway became more efficient and cooperative because the entire city became more efficient and cooperative.

Furthermore, that cooperative spirit was not motivated by the statistics of traffic engineers but by a great deal of inspiration and sacrifice: families went on vacations, local communities decided not to mind the noise of the truckers after dark. Affect was also a crucial factor. One need only recall the joy that the Olympic games bring to a city or, as Seale mentions, the fear that kept many people off the freeway or scared them into vacations out of the city.

The Cooperative Principle of Freeway Driving

The problem of traffic congestion cannot be solved by a few isolated technical policies that keep drivers off the road. For the freeways to work as smoothly as they did during the Olympics, the city of Los Angeles must maintain a level of inspired cooperation all year round. That seems unlikely.

The limitations of Roper's suggestion can be exposed further by Thomas C. Schelling, who in his book <u>Micromotives and Macrobehavior</u> discusses how human systems maintain equilibrium. Schelling argues that many human systems cannot be permanently efficient because the more efficient they become, the more they attract additional people who diminish that efficiency. Schelling's freeway examples are particularly relevant here. For instance, he argues that traffic helicopters, which report accidents and blockages on congested freeways and recommend alternative routes, actually do more harm than good. It would be better for most drivers, he says, if no one knew which freeways were moving the smoothest; such knowledge only motivates drivers to converge there and reduce efficiency. And rather that having one inefficient freeway and several efficient ones, all routes now become equally congested.

Schelling provides another example that makes it doubtful that the freeway efficiency during the Olympics could be replicated. Let us say, he says, that the traffic helicopter or highway engineers warn nearly every driver away from a particular route. Let us also imagine that a few drivers who ignore this warning find that rout quite efficient. If those who took alternative routes or stayed home discovered this fact, they would be unlikely to heed the warning the second time, converging on the area and creating the catastrophe that traffic engineers originally predicted. The Olympics case was analogous. Those drivers who were warned away from Los Angeles or the freeways because the media images of terrible congestion would not be so frightened the second time. Nor would adopting the Olympic policies year-round, even if possible, solve all traffic problems. As Schelling points out, making a freeway efficient makes it more attractive, thus increasing its appeal and thereby diminishing its efficiency (1978:115).

Schelling's work suggests that contrary to the engineering model, improving traffic flow demands a focus on drivers—their motivations, attitudes, and beliefs—as well as vehicle flow. However, traffic engineers generally promote solutions—such as <u>ridesharing</u>—that ignore the human and social dimensions of driving. Although ridesharing appears a good idea, there are many social reasons why it is not popular or practical. Some of these reasons are discussed by Chadwick Thayer, a commuter, who appeared on a recent radio talk-show on traffic. He and his wife one ride-shared but no longer do because, he says,

> It was taking up too much time because she would have to fight the traffic plus also wait for a ride and she has a personal life to lead, too; she'd like to go to the store, or whatever; so we got a motorcycle so she's got the car and now she can handle her own running around (Thayer 1986).

While Thayer's opinion is not a professional one, it does clearly include some rational reasons not to rideshare. He reminds us that people do not commute merely to arrive at work or home in the most efficient way. Commuting is a social activity, and altering one's daily schedules and priorities to rideshare demands a sacrifice that many people are unable or unwilling to make. It is also a sacrifice that cannot be inspired through statistics alone. Even though everyone may know that ridesharing is a good thing—like exercise or eating vegetables—everyone is not convinced enough to adopt the practice.

Traffic engineers are therefore destined to be disappointed by the simple fact that freeway driving is a complex activity that cannot be accounted for merely by statistical evidence or by calculating optimal vehicle flow. As Donald Taylor (1981) puts it, "Design engineers, too, should show anger and irritation at the way carefully-designed man-machine systems are 'misused' with what seems like deliberate carelessness. It can seem almost as if the public is out to defeat safety measures by finding new ways of having accidents in an increasingly safer world" (488). What this thesis argues, of course, is that what seems like perversity or carelessness to traffic engineers may not be so at all.

The Solitary Driver Model: People Without a System

As the last section demonstrates, the primary barriers to implementing the mechanistic model on a full scale are simply human emotions, idiosyncrasies, and social pressures. Yet these are the precise dimensions of driving that mechanistic accounts of driving ignore. They are ignored for two reasons. The first is that they challenge the rational model of human behavior upon which mechanistic traffic models depend. Yet while many of the psychological studies of traffic supplement (and sometimes contradict) the mechanistic models, they do contain another weakness, as the following review plans to show.

Most psychological studies of traffic focus on the individual psychology of drivers without understanding their relations to other drivers. Whereas the mechanistic model discusses the driving system by ignoring the individual, many of these psychological studies focus on individuals—their neuroses or character type—and ignore the system in which they must perform.

For example, there have been numerous studies on the suicidal tendencies of individual drivers (Crancer and Quiring, 1968; Litman and Tabachnick, 1967; Osman, 1968; Tabachnick, Gussen, Litman, Peck, Tiber and Wold, 1973; Kennedy, Phanjoo and Shekim, 1971).

Other researchers have looked at the adjustment problems of drivers (e.g. Brenner and Selzer, 1969; Crancer and Quiring, 1969a; Crancer and Quiring, 1969b; Eelkema, Brousseau, Koshnik and McGee, 1970; McMurray, 1968; Schmidt, Perlin, Towns, Fisher and Shaffer, 1972) and accident proneness (Shaw and Sichel, 1971). Still other investigators have looked at the socialization problems of drivers (Andersson, Nilsson and Hendricksson, 1970; Carlson and Klein, 1970; Klein 1968, 1972). While these studies are important for demonstrating how individual affect and mental health may complicate the driving task, they tend to separate the subjects of study from their interactions with other drivers and the driving system.

The dominant psychological model that informs traffic studies remains the behavioral. An excellent description of this model of driving is presented by Ray Fuller, in his essay "A conceptualization of driving behavior as threat avoidance." Fuller states:

> Compared with most other things we do, driving has a high potential for aversive consequences. To achieve his or her travel objective a driver cannot simply select a suitable heading and speed and then sit back and keep watch. Once in motion he/she must continuously and actively make adjustments not only to attain some desired travel objective (i.e. a particular destination, usually within a particular time period) but also to avoid aversive stimuli or situations such as driving off the roadway, losing control of the vehicle or colliding with another road user (McGlade 1970, Parsons 1976, 1979, Risk 1981).

The behavioral model begins by assuming that the motivating factor of safe driving is a negative one, an avoidance of threat, precautions to the dangerous aversive possibilities in the driving task. Safe driving, it implies, is motivated by fear.

The two most dominant psychological models of driving behavior are Wilde's Theory of Risk Homeostasis (Wilde 1981) and the Zero-risk model of driver behavior proposed by Naatanen and Summala (1974, 1976). We shall review these models in turn.

Wilde's theory of risk homeostasis posits that drivers drive in such a way to maintain a comfortable level of anxiety about the fear of accident or arrests. Drivers thus make adjustments in their driving habits to reduce the chance of risk to this internalized level. However, Wilde stresses, that the level of risk is never completely reduces; drivers will feel comfortable at a certain level somewhere above zero. This fact is significant because it means the level of risk homeostasis is constantly changing.

What changes it? Wilde says that if driving does not provide the evidence that caution is needed, then drivers will essentially increase their ability to feel comfortable, even though their behavior is unsafe. In fact, the level of risk increases, says Wilde, until some driving experience—like an accident or close call—reminds drivers of the need for caution, thus forcing them to reduce their risky driving to a level at which they are comfortable. Wilde (1976) states that "accident tolls and caution relate to one another in a compensatory function."

More recently, (Wilde 1981), Wilde argues that safe driving is motivated not merely by the desire to maintain a comfortable level of anxiety but by the desire to avoid a level that exceeds comfort. In both models, Wilde posits that driving behavior that is determined by anxiety, or fear. His recommendations for safety programs, then, would be to remind drivers of the dangers of certain practices, such as driving without a seat belt and so on.

Naatanen and Sunnula (1976), while maintaining the behaviorist paradigms, have designed a model slightly different from Wilde's. Unlike Wilde, they do not believe that the acceptable level of risk changes; they hold that it is zero most of the time. They do not assume that the subjective risk is altered by a general sense of caution, but believe that it is overrun by more important motivations ("extra motives") during the driving task. For instance, the fear of being late for work may be more intense than the fear of risking a dangerous driving behavior. Hence, subjective risk is suppressed or pushed to its maximum threshold. Safety programs, therefore, say Naatanen and Summula, should have one goal: lowering the threshold of the driver's subjective risk. They state:

> In general, the present model suggests that the subjective-risk reactions of road users constitute an important determinant of decision making and behavior on the road, counteracting the behavioral tendencies associated with the existing generally excitatory kinds of motives (1976, 189-190).

As can be seen from these examples, the basic strategy of behaviorist approaches to driving is to determine the motivations for safe driving and then to establish ways to motivate that behavior. While the behavioral model is important because it reminds us of the risk involved in driving, it suffers from two shortcomings. The first is that it does not account for the way different people react to the risk of driving. Secondly, its emphasis on safety makes it inadequate when dealing with freeway driving, where the goal is often efficiency rather than safety. For example, all behavioral models of driving consider speeding an unsafe act, even though freeway driving often requires one to exceed the legal limit to maintain the flow of traffic.

Ray Fuller (1984), though a behaviorist, counters much of the behavioral model by arguing that the stimuli that motivate safe driving are not static and therefore cannot be manipulated by law officers or safety programs. All stimuli in the environment, he argues, must be seen as having only aversive <u>potential</u>:

> Stimuli in the road environment are rarely intrinsically aversive but become so only as a result of the <u>interaction</u> between what the road user does and properties of the stimuli themselves. Generally it is the driver's own actions which determine whether or not his or her interactions with the road environment will be punishing (1143).

If as Fuller argues, drivers are not automatically motivated into safe behavior, there appears support for a model of driving that stresses the interpretation that drivers must make. But because Fuller remains in the behaviorist paradigm, he must arrive at different reasons for the fact that stimuli in the roadway are only potentially aversive. What determines the status of the stimuli is not the driver's interpretation but the "driver's own actions," the style of the driver, his or her personality types and cognitive or affective style. This last factor, the style of the driver, is the most important, according to Fuller.

Thus, Fuller distinguishes two primary types of drivers: there are those who practice "anticipatory avoidance driving," which means they are preadaptive, more introverted, and are sensitive to cognitive approaches to road safety propaganda; and those who practice "delayed avoidance driving," which means they are post adaptive, tolerate greater risk, are more extraverted, and are sensitive to emotional approaches in road safety propaganda. The goal is to transform the latter drivers into the former, a goal that could be met, Fuller says, with the following suggestion: beginning drivers need to "learn the precursors of hazards and to develop the association between discriminative stimuli and potential aversive stimuli." And where are these lessons learned? Not in the classroom but in "direct experiences of contingencies, particularly of near misses, narrow escapes and, unfortunately, accidents, when unsafe responses have been made" (1146).

Behavioral models, in short, are based on the importance of subjective risk—the fear of accident or arrest that serves as the prime motivation of safe and legal driving. Despite the differences between Wilde, Naatanen and Summula, and Fuller, their models share the assumption that subjective risk determines the choices that drivers make. Therefore, it must be the goal of safety campaigns to motivate drivers by lowering their threshold of tolerable risk and by teaching them avoidance behavior.

Expressive Driving

The primary shortcomings of behavioral models are 1) that they treat drivers as relatively passive <u>reactors</u> to stimuli rather than thinking <u>actors</u>, 2) that they limit the motivations for safe driving behavior to the protection of self or "narcissistic homeostasis", 3) that, like mechanistic models, they see driving as a solitary activity, and 4) that they assume the only reason to drive is instrumental. For Fuller, for example, the driver's instrumental goal—arriving at a certain place in a certain amount of time—is primary; other matters are extraneous.

Several studies, however, do stress the expressive as well as instrumental motivation to drive. Ralph Bolton, in a study entitled "Machismo in Motion: the Ethos of Peruvian Truckers," brings some of the expressive and communicative functions of driving to light. Existing studies are limited, Bolton says, because they ignore this fact:

> Motor vehicles obviously have narrowly-defined instrumental functions, transferring people and goods in a rapid and efficient manner from one place to another. Less obvious, perhaps, is the tremendous importance of expressive aspects of the travel and transportation complex.... All too often the expressive aspects of material good and technology are regarded as trivial, when in fact they may be of fundamental significance.

By studying the kinds of messages that Peruvian truck drivers place on their vehicles, Bolton was able to demonstrate that truck drivers express many feelings while driving—such as anger, rage, desire, and power—in ways that would be socially unacceptable if they were not driving. The details of his study are not as significant as his conclusion, which is that much driving behavior is an act of communication to impress others. Driving, for the subjects of Bolton's study, was a crucial part of the driver's sense of self.

Studies like Bolton's can often explain driving phenomena that the behavioral model cannot, such as speeding. Fuller (1981), for instance, considers speeding a personal pleasure that comes from the desire for arousal, a pleasure that competes with the pleasure of feeling safe: "A competing response of high speed, for instance, may itself be rewarding because it increases arousal to a more satisfactory level; because it is experienced as exhilarating or because it conforms to norms for speed, perceived by the driver" (1144). Still, Fuller does not explain <u>why</u> people speed. While the instrumental reason may be to arrive at a desired location in less time, there are also expressive reasons for speeding that the behaviorist model ignores.

Bolton's study allows us to view speeding in a much larger context. Citing the work of traffic psychologist Roberts (1972), Bolton reminds us that driving is an opportunity for a self test, a chance to put one's ego on the line among other drivers. Roberts states that while driving, "Hazards and risks are omnipresent; errors can be fatal. By successfully overcoming the repetitive challenges confronting him, a driver may enhance his feelings of power and competence" (Bolton 399). With Bolton's study as background, one can see the act of speeding in other than behavioral terms; it is not pleasurable, as Fuller argues, merely because it can arouse the driver, but it is also pleasurable because it gives the driver a sense of power. The arousal has an interpersonal dimension. Speeding is a social act.

Driving as a Road Warrior

As Bolton's study suggests, driving is not merely a solitary act. Drivers often choose certain behavior, like speeding, for the expressed purpose of impressing or dominating other drivers. Such a phenomenon brings up the important issue of competitiveness on the roadway, a competitiveness that has come to be described in increasingly militaristic terms. Freeway driving, implies two recent Los Angeles writers, turns one into a "Road Warrior" (Seale 1986; Balter 1986).

Feeling competitive toward other drivers is well known to everyone, especially on the freeway, where other drivers are considered a hindrance. It is common to wish that all *other* drivers would take alternative routes, rideshare, use public transportation, or, in general, disappear. The general frustration with other drivers sometimes perpetuates the illusion that the freeway system would work best if one were the only driver.

The reasons for competitiveness on the highway are not studied in any detail. However, the ideal of the solitary driver, which is perpetuated in the media, probably has some effect. Television advertisements for new cars typically show a solitary driver enjoying his or her freedom on the road away from other vehicles. When other drivers appear in advertising, they are usually impediments which, like trees in the road, allow the technology of the new vehicle to be demonstrated. Traffic safety slogans like "Watch Out for the Other Guy" or "Drive Defensively" also perpetuate the idea that driving is a solitary activity and that other drivers are a danger to one's safety.

While on might expect these popular accounts—whose influence cannot be underestimated—to promote a simplistic view of driving, the idea that driving is a solitary, competitive act also appears quite dominant in the scholarly literature. John Cohen, for example, in his book <u>Behavior in Uncertainty</u> (Cohen 1964) states the competitive aspect of driving rather poetically:

> Every motorist or motor cyclist finds himself in a competitive situation, a contest, where the outcome, his individual triumph and superiority, turns on whether he can drive faster than his fellow, elbow him out or otherwise outwit him. His vehicle becomes for him a symbol of his own body, and he may have no other outlet for asserting his prowess. A man at the wheel is visible, as it were, through a high-powered magnifying glass. With a minute expenditure of energy, he can demonstrate his manhood and virility. Others—the horseman, the cyclist, the man in space, even the traveler on British Railways—enjoy speed, but no one can run amok like the motorist, by the gentlest pressure of his toes on the accelerator (1964:64-65).

Cohen goes so far as to blame this quality of driving on the driving act itself and not on the individual personality, a genuine difference from most psychological studies: he says that driving can transform even a "timid and peaceful citizen into a beast of prey" (Cohen 1964:63).

The most cogent discussion of the "egocentricity of the driving pattern" appears in Bliersbach and Dellen's "Interaction Conflicts and Interaction Patterns in Traffic Situations" (1980). Like Bolton and Cohen, they discuss the expressive aspects of driving that most studies ignore, but unlike them, they do not contain the affective and expressive dimensions of driving to rage and competitiveness. Instead, they see a spectrum of driving patterns, which represent different ego states of drivers. Six primary patterns of driving emerge from their study:

1. The pattern of the thrill.
2. The pattern of the power display.
3. The pattern of self-testing.
4. The pattern of smoothly driving along.
5. The pattern of piloting, and
6. The pattern of exchanging insults. (335).

The most important dimension of their study for this discussion is their findings that despite traffic campaigns that tell drivers to feel friendly and neighborly toward one another, most drivers still see driving as a solitary task, where the existence of other drivers is seen as an obstacle, a hindrance, or a danger. And it is this basic "egocentricity" of driving, they conjecture, that explains why drivers feel "anger and rage" when other drivers interfere with their transportation goals, and why this anger is always fixed on the other driver, and not relativized by considering the intentions of others." According to their study, most drivers interviewed saw it as nearly impossible to consider the point of view of other drivers. They state that "There exists a permanent suspicion that the other driver intends to hinder you (or do you down)." Furthermore, it is the egocentricity of the driver that explains why drivers are "easy to insult" (334).

Other studies have tried to understand the competitive aspects of driving, the fact that drivers keep their hostile feelings close to the surface, and are "easy to insult." Mentzos (1976) takes this phenomena as evidence that driving is an instrument of "narcissistic homeostasis" to which others represent a constant threat. As Michael Balter describes it:

> For many L.A. drivers, being forced to hit the brakes while cruising down a six-lane freeway is akin to a personal insult., an affront to their sense of independence and mobility (Balter, 1986:20).

The idea that driving is a solitary, competitive act where other drivers only endanger and insult one is very common in both the popular and scholarly literature. The challenge of a cooperative model of driving must be to explain this phenomenon in other terms. The beginning of that challenge must be a review of alternative accounts to driving that expose the positive expressive functions of driving and the cooperative system that underlies the relation between drivers. It is to these studies that we now turn.

Toward an Interpretive Model of Driving: A Critique of the Mechanistic and Behavioral Models

Currently, the most comprehensive accounts of driving behavior are not in psychology but in hermeneutics, sociology, and philosophy. Nevertheless, these discussions are important because they explicitly demonstrate the limitations of the strict mechanistic, behaviorist, and gestalt models.

In his iconoclastic article, "The Hermeneutics of Accidents and Safety," Donald H. Taylor challenges the existing "ergonomic" model of driving. Ergonomics is the science that studies the man-machine systems, the machine-like qualities of man, and concerns itself with deterministic, ultimately predictable scientific descriptions. While the ergonomic model has been very influential and explains a great deal, Taylor argues that it cannot explain certain important driving phenomenon, such as accidents. It cannot explain accidents, Taylor says, because driving is a highly interpretive activity where drivers are constantly interpreting the meanings and effects of their actions and those of others. Accidents, on the other hand, are "meaningless." They are what Taylor calls "black holes of meaning," and are incomprehensible to drivers who have not experienced them directly.

The ergonomic model of traffic safety, however, tries to use accidents as motivators for safe driving. Ergonomic models try to posit different causes of accidents, such as speeding, drunk driving, not wearing seat belts, not having brakes checked, and so on. But, Taylor argues, drivers are unimpressed with this attempt to find a "cause" to a "meaningless" event like an accident which ahs no cause. So that while statistics may show that some of the above practices prevent accidents, they are not the entire reason. The fact is that most drivers have violated some of these safety practices at one time or another and <u>not</u> had an accident. As Taylor puts it, "It is difficult to link the antecedents with their consequences, because exactly similar events can lead to widely different consequences" (491).

Because of the limitations of the ergonomic model, a model which underlies both the mechanistic and behavioral approach to driving, Taylor argues that a "hermeneutical," or interpretive, model of driving is needed. Such a model would consider drivers not as passive beings who react to stimuli but as active seekers after meaning. Taylor calls for studies of driving that are less interested in objective criteria and more concerned with how drivers interpret events. The difference between Taylor's approach and existing models can be summarized in the following statement:

> As Winch (1958) argued, it is not possible to deduce the meanings of actions merely by observing them, i.e. by regarding them as behavior. It is this, more than anything, which separates hermeneutical enquiry from conventional science. The meanings of actions have to be interpreted in the light of the agents' motives, purposes, principles and beliefs, indeed from the whole social context in which the actions take place (492).

In his argument that behavioral models of traffic psychology will never be sufficient, Taylor cites psychologists Gauld and Shotter (1977). They argue that viewing humans as generalized machines cannot explain important aspects of human behavior that psychologists should study:

> It has been proposed that the psychological and social sciences are essentially hermeneutical, that the proper task of the psychologist is not to formulate the laws of human behavior, but to elucidate the "meanings" of pieces of human behavior (25).

And in response to the fact that many psychologists consider qualitative analysis to be merely poor quantitative work, he cites Shotter (1980) who warns that "We forget...that what matters most is that people learn what it is to take responsibility for their actions... without that determination, that kind of self control, there can be no guarantee of order in the community at all" (21).

Shotter's statement should sound particularly familiar to psychotherapists, who see their goal as practically helping people to take responsibility for their lives, rather than trying to explain them or lay down rules of behavior. Furthermore, Taylor's hermeneutic model of driving is fully compatible with psychotherapy, as evidenced by his closing his paper by another quote from Shotter:

The truth about people, about human nature, then, is not something that is awaiting discovery, ready made, like something under a stone on a beach: it can only be made by people in dialogue, as the product of a social act, in continual mutual interrogation and reply (1975,135).

A Cooperative Model of Driving: People Working in Systems

As the previous discussion shows, most models of driving ignore the psycho-social dimensions of driving. However, there are a few scholars who see the driver as a member of society and driving as a subsystem of everyday life. Their findings and models of human behavior are particularly relevant to establishing a cooperative model. The goal of this final section, therefore, is to discuss the research that helps us to see driving as a rule-governed, cooperative, cultural system that engages the driver as a psycho-social being, not merely as a law-abiding man-machine.

I would like to begin directly with the usefulness of the gestalt model of psychology.

The Gestalt of Driving in a System

One of the main reasons that the solitary and competitive model of driving is perpetuated is that most traffic psychologists have not brought psycho-social models to understanding the driving task. Most studies tend to emphasize the independence and autonomy of the individual driver. While these studies are certainly important, they tell us little about the aspect of driving that require intense cooperation among drivers, such as freeway driving. Even many gestalt psychologists who write about traffic concentrate on the system's effect on the driver and not the interdependence of driver and system. Mentzos' description of driving as "narcissistic homeostasis" is typical of gestalt accounts that focus on what happens inside cars rather than among them (Mentzos, 1980). However, gestalt psychology does not need to be treated reductively; on the contrary, there are several gestalt principles that allow us to view the freeway as a gestalt in its own right.

As Fritz Perls explains, Gestalt psychology is based on the premise that all behavior of an organism is governed by the drive for homeostasis, "the process by which the organism maintains its equilibrium and therefore its health under varying conditions" (Perls, 1973,4). The gestalt approach not only unifies the mind and body, but it emphasizes that human beings are in constant interaction with the environment Perls states:

> The environment and the organism stand in a relationship of mutuality to one another. Neither is the victim of the other. Their relationship is actually that of dialectical opposites. To satisfy its needs, the organism has to find its required supplements in the environment (1973,17).

Gestalt psychology offers us one way of understanding the complex interactions and counterbalances of the freeway system, especially if we notice how Gestalt psychology is used to understand human groups, such as families, through General Living Systems Theory. Systems Theory is explained by James Grier Miller:

> General Systems theory asserts that the universe is composed of a hierarchy of concrete systems, defined as accumulations of matter and energy organized into co-acting, interrelated subsystems or components and existing in a common space-time continuum. It provides a conceptual framework within which the content of biological and social sciences can be unified. It seeks to eliminate the firm disciplinary boundaries that obscure the orderly relationships among parts of the real world and lead many to overlook their shared characteristics (Miller 1978).

Gestalt approaches to family therapy have many parallels with a gestalt approach to freeways. Family therapy based on the gestalt model considers the family as a group of individuals functioning interdependently in a system. Thus, the importance of wholeness is maintained, but the wholeness is the unity of a system rather than of individuals. Family therapy based on the gestalt extends the notion of wholeness: "Every part of a system is so related to its fellow parts that a change in one part inevitably causes a change in other parts and in the whole system" (3). Like the family, the freeway must be considered as an open system that can accommodate constant readjustment for the needs of others.

Freeway Driving as Culture

THE COOPERATIVE PRINCIPLE OF FREEWAY DRIVING

Understanding the importance of freeway driving as a cultural event, especially in Los Angeles, is crucial if we are to fully account for the driving experience. As Ralph Bolton states,

> It is nonetheless apparent to anyone who has ever traveled in a foreign culture that there are significant differences as well as similarities in drivers and driving behavior cross-culturally. Rules of the road vary to some extent from country to country, but differences in driving behavior stem from differences in general behavioral style as well as from such rule differences. Cultural differences in action style undoubtedly influence driving behavior (Bolton, 314).

While the American highway culture has been studied in some depth by Roberts and his colleagues, who distinguished between "concourse" and "tube" culture (Roberts, Kozelka, and Arth, 1956), the cultural values of Los Angeles freeway driving are only now becoming apparent. The general opinion of writers and commentators is that the freeway is now the essential cultural experience of living in Los Angeles. The following extended quotation, which appeared in <u>Commentary</u> magazine (January 1986), makes this point explicitly:

> As for Los Angeles, the essential problem—apart from the "There's no <u>there</u> there" issue—is Hollywood. Understanding Hollywood is crucial to understanding American popular culture, and thus American, but Hollywood's importance is much too generalized to be uniquely the property of Los Angeles. What is left is the freeway system. Driving on it, Joan Didion writes, is "the only secular communion Los Angeles has." Yes, writes David Brodsly in <u>LA Freeway:</u>

<u>An</u> <u>Appreciative Essay</u>: "Every time we merge with traffic we join our community in a wordless creed: the belief in individual freedom, in a technological liberation from place and circumstance, in a democracy of personal mobility... The LA freeway is the cathedral of its time and place." Yes, yes, writes Christopher Knight, reviewing the preceding in <u>Public Interest</u>: "The secular theology of this New Eden is enacted in the creed spoken in the automotive basilica." But wait, says Bret Easton Ellis in his novel <u>Less Than Zero</u>, "People are afraid to merge on freeways in Los Angeles." So, it is that of Los Angeles the less said the better and the more said the sillier.

Laying the author's negative attitude toward Los Angeles aside, this quotation provides several significant perceptions of freeway driving in this city: the first is that it is a communal activity, which means that people driving have a sense of the others beside them that is not necessarily hostile; the second is that this "communion" is a difficult experience for some people, namely the intimidated drivers whom we have discussed earlier, the third perception is the fact that Los Angeles freeway drivers consider their driving to more than instrumental; it is an expression of their identity.

The cultural value that Los Angeles drivers attach to the efficiency of the freeway is crucial to understanding the intense reactions of these drivers to congestion. If driving the freeway represents being free, mobile, independent, and outdoors, being trapped on the freeway means a great deal more than being late for a destination. We can suppose that this frustration means more to Los Angeles drivers than it might to drivers in other cities, where the "toll way," "highway," or "interstate," is merely for instrumental purposes, or in cities where congested is to be expected.

The Cooperative Principle of Freeway Driving

The fact is that congestion in Los Angeles is not a tradition; it seems like a challenge to the entire lifestyle of freeway drivers. Congestion on the "freeway" becomes a contradiction in terms. One cannot be free when others are blocking one's path. As Rugoff describes it:

> When traffic is reduced to a vicious stop-and-go dribble, that utopian vision of Los Angeles vanishes in the exhaust of a million stuttering automobiles. Rush hour betrays the promise of the freeway, transforming it into something more like a prison than an escape route. Car pooling and public transportation—the only real cures for automotive arteriosclerosis—effectively nullify L.A.'s libertarian raison d'etre. And building more freeways won't solve the problem—the record shows over and over again that increased freeway capacity only generates more use. Evidently the freeway doesn't simply answer needs, it creates them (21).

Rugoff's statement articulates what we have emphasized so far in this chapter:

1) That freeway driving in Los Angeles represents a psycho-socio-cultural experience,
2) The drivers in Los Angeles expect more from driving than mere transportation; other motivations for a smooth freeway exist,
3) That the frustration of freeway congestion is extremely stressful, and
4) That fewer cars or more freeways will not solve the problem; somehow the cooperation among drivers and among citizens must be improved.

We have also seen that only a few models of the driving task can explain all of these dimensions. In the next chapter, a cooperative model will be developed that tries to account for dimensions that have been ignored.

Chapter III

Design of the Study

Introduction

Most studies of driving ignore the psychology of the drivers; those that do not concentrate on the individual driver and ignore the fact that freeway driving is a system with "specific field conditions" (Sporli 1978; cited in Bliersbach and Dellen 1980). By studying the freeway as a human system, individual drivers become less important than how they cooperate with other drivers. These cooperative interactions must be explored and analyzed if we are ever to understand how to make driving more efficient (Wilde 1980).

However, as we have seen, attempts to describe the relations between drivers are more concerned with the "competitive" or "hostile" dimensions, as emphasis that merely perpetuates the alienation that most people feel. Bliersbach and Dellen remark that "A driver who does not expect any help or co-operation from other drivers does not feel an inclination to co-operate with other drivers: he drives, literally, alone" (484).

Yet, while the drivers in Bliersbach and Dellen's study may have felt "alone," the fact is that such a phenomenon cannot really exist, especially if we consider the highway as a system. Regardless of whether other drivers are present on the roadway or not, their existence constitutes the complex transportation system, a system which includes the Department of Motor Vehicles, the legal infrastructure, and fellow taxpayers. Of course, when other drivers are present, the need for a cooperative system becomes even more present. The cooperative system that underlies the perceived solitary and competitive experience of driving will be made explicit in this chapter.

Hypothesis

It is my hypothesis that a cooperative model of freeway driving can explain the stressful and anti-social behavior of freeway drivers and the unsafe and inefficient freeway conditions that result.

Definition of Terms

Model: A model is an idealized description of a process that accounts for a phenomena or a pattern of practices; it determines what aspects of the phenomenon are highlighted or excluded. A model of freeway driving tries to account for the experience of driving. "A model," says Thomas C. Schelling, can be a precise and economical statement of a set of relationships that are sufficient to produce the phenomenon in question. Or, a model can be an actual biological, mechanical, or social system that embodies the relationships in an especially transparent way" (Shelling 1978:83).

Implicature: An implicature means literally "what is implied." It is also a term used by H.P. Grice to identify a meaningful violation of expectation, meaningful because it forces us to interpret the event in a new way. If that expectation is cooperation, and a violation occurred, that violation would create an implicature, the meaning of the violation (Grice 1967:15).

Assumptions

1. That freeway driving demands an intense cooperation among drivers.
2. That freeway interactions can be seen as a subsystem of social interactions.
3. That traffic safety campaigns base their suggestions on theoretical models of traffic psychology.
4. That understanding the cooperative nature of freeway driving can make a person a safer and more efficient driver.

Scope and Limitations

My study describes the models—or idealized descriptions—from which traffic specialists work when they try to 1) understand freeway phenomena or 2) recommend strategies for making the freeway safe and efficient. I focus on the models of these specialists because understanding the model by which traffic specialists view the driving task makes it easier to see the differences between their ideas of how driving should work and how it actually does work. In this study, I examine specifically the ways that current models of driving ignore the psycho-social dimensions of the activity.

The Los Angeles freeway system is chosen as my primary area of study for several reasons. First, my own experience of freeway driving comes from this area, and my study was motivated by frustrations that I have felt while driving local freeways. Second, the Los Angeles freeway system is world-renowned for its length (over 700 miles) and its complexity. Finally, the freeway is becoming known as the central cultural artifact of Los Angeles life.

The freeway itself is chosen as a focus because the freeway system is the best place to clearly identify the cooperative nature of driving in action. Although the dynamics that I describe are not absent on surface streets, the freeway presents these dynamics in a concentrated form. One can literally observe the dynamics of cooperative behavior and the consequences of non-cooperative behavior. There is perhaps no place else where so many people are engaged in a group process and where each individual is responsible for the outcome. Moreover, compared to surface streets, whose driving requirements are somewhat restricted by laws and boundaries, the freeway demands more active interpretation and judgment.

The limitations of my study include a lack of appropriate empirical data. But this limitation is more significant to the consequence of the study that to the study itself. Even though a cooperative model may explain the freeway driving system in the abstract, traffic engineers and state officials would be interested in empirical data that justifies my conclusions. Perhaps some of this data can be supplied by future studies. My study is also challenged by the many studies that show that drivers do not feel cooperative, that, in fact, they feel competitive and solitary. And while my study does explain these feelings as reactions to the violations of cooperation, the feelings of drivers cannot be ignored. These feelings deserve more careful study than can be provided here. Toward the end, however, I do make several suggestions for how these feelings can be explored and expressed within an alternative traffic school program.

My study is also slightly limited by the lack of specific data about Los Angeles drivers. The most influential work in traffic psychology comes from other cultures and other cities. And while I presume that many of these generalizations apply cross culturally, there may be significant differences in cultures that challenge the universality of the cooperative model. Nonetheless, even if that is so, the cooperative model can be used as an initial measure by which other hypotheses about driving can be made.

Procedure

A cooperative model or theory of driving will be articulated and the explanatory power of the model will be tested against accounts of driving phenomena from both scientific and popular domains.

Data Gathering

The data that will test the cooperative model comes from two different domains. The first is traffic psychology. There are several studies by traffic psychologists in which driving phenomena are presented and explained. These studies were selected because of their influence on the field of traffic psychology and on government officials who establish driving policy. The two psychological approaches whose data will be used are the behaviorist model and the psycho-social.

The second domain from which I gather my data comes from studies outside the field of traffic psychology. My contention is that the explanatory power of the cooperative model is made clear if it accounts for not only scientific data but for driving phenomena that most drivers experience every day. Toward that end, several driving phenomena will be described, including the limitations of laws to create better driving and the recent controversy over the "Baby on Board" caution signs.

Articulating the Cooperative Model: Theoretical Foundations

The foundation for the theory of cooperative freeway driving comes from philosopher H. Paul Grice's model of the <u>cooperative principle</u>. According to Grice (1967), all rational and beneficial social interactions between people include expectations of cooperation. These expectations are not conscious. They are tacitly assumed in each interaction where rational social behavior is needed, for example, in Grice's study, during conversation. The <u>cooperative principle</u> states that you should:

> Make your contribution such as is required, at the stage at which it occurs, by the accepted purpose or direction of the exchange in which you are engaged.

Grice emphasizes that contributions must be timely and <u>appropriate</u> to the activity at hand. But he does not limit the cooperative principle to conversation, since he sees the rules of conversation as representing rules of cooperative rational behavior in general: "The observance of the cooperative principles and the maxims, in a talk exchange, could be thought of as a quasi-contractual matter, with parallels outside the realm of discourse" (1967:48). The example Grice uses is working on the vehicle with a friend: if I ask you for a wrench and you give me a hammer, I realize that my expectations of cooperation have been violated.

At first it might seem that Grice is merely positing a rational paradise much as the traffic engineers do, or that his theory contradicts the fact that drivers <u>do not feel cooperative</u> on the freeways (Mentzos 1976; Bliersbach and Dellen 1981). But neither perception is correct.

Grice states that we can only understand "irrational" or "competitive" behavior if we see it as a violation of rational cooperative behavior.

The <u>cooperative principle</u> does not assert that people always cooperate, only that we <u>expect</u> cooperation from them. The fact is, they often do not cooperate; they violate cooperation intentionally. Yet these violations are not meaningless, nor are they breakdowns in communication. They are, on the contrary, significant acts. Grice describes these "meaningful violations of cooperation" with the term <u>implicature</u>, which means what is implies. An <u>implicature</u> occurs when the expectation is violated. So in the example above, when I ask for a wrench and you give me a hammer, the implicature is likely to be that I am so clumsy at auto mechanics that the hammer would be about as useful as a wrench. How I interpret this implication (Do I consider it a joke, an insult, a means of shaming me, or do I consider you an idiot?) reveals a great deal about my psycho-social behavior.

The Cooperative Principle of Freeway Driving

The cooperative principle of driving is precisely the same as that of any rational and beneficial activity. Participants are expected to make their contributions "such as required, at the stage at which it occurs, by the accepted purpose or directions of the exchange." And while the purpose of driving on surface streets may vary—some may which to arrive swiftly, others may enjoy sight-seeing—the purpose of driving on the freeway is fairly clear. That purpose can be stated in a precise principle:

> <u>To be cooperative on the freeway, drive as safely and swiftly as possible under the conditions.</u>

These expectations can be defined in terms of two maxims: while driving the freeway one is expected to <u>Be safe</u> and <u>Be swift</u>.

We recall that the importance of the cooperative principle is not that everyone is cooperative; on the contrary, by realizing the underlying expectations of participants in an activity, the meaning of the violations of cooperation become clear. Let us now consider how these maxims explain the frustrations on the freeway.

The maxim <u>Be safe</u> means that drivers are expected to drive in a way that guarantees the safety of themselves and others. When this maxim is violated on the freeway, say by a driver who tailgates or cuts in front of us, the implication is that this driver does not care about our safety. It also implies that he or she does not care about our existence. Because a violation of the <u>Be safe</u> maxim places our lives in jeopardy and diminishes our self worth, it is easy to understand why such violations are met with anger and hostility. The second maxim, <u>Be swift</u>, is violated mostly when traffic is congested. During congested periods, we expect drivers to take every opportunity to increase the speed of the freeway. When drivers do not, such as when they do not "full the gaps: in other lanes, or when they stop and gape too long at an accident, the implication is that they are not interested in keeping the traffic moving. This violation is often met with general frustration.

Indeed, the cooperative principle of driving allows us to understand the folk wisdom of the statement that "Those who drive faster than us are maniacs and those who drive slower are idiots." More importantly, the cooperative principle allows us to understand why drivers often express feelings during driving that would not be socially acceptable in other situations. In short, the cooperative model allows us to understand why drivers cooperate and what happens when they do not.

In sum, we begin with the premise that drivers expect cooperation from other drivers; in fact, they would probably not enter the highways if they did not. Specifically, they expect others to follow the two maxims <u>Be safe</u> and <u>Be swift</u>. Violations of this expectation create implicatures, most of which are interpreted as hostile gestures, which often motivates more hostility, more implicatures and so on.

The Consequences of Violating Cooperation

The fact is, when cooperation is violated on the freeway, two different consequences result; one for the individual driver, who suffers an "upset," and the other for the freeway system, whose efficiency and cooperation is significantly reduced. While these consequences are interdependent, they can be briefly described in their different dimensions.

When a driver interprets a lack of cooperation from another driver, an "upset" occurs. Werner Erhard provides a useful definition of "upset": "To disturb the functioning, fulfillment, or completion of; to disturb mentally or emotionally, or physically make sick; to overturn or overthrow, especially unexpectedly." Since a major cause of an upset, says Erhard, is the "unfulfilled expectation," the freeway must be seen as a potential breeding ground for personal upset.

This individual upset also affects the efficiency of the whole freeway system. Often times, one uncooperative act will create another uncooperative act in its wake. When this happens, the freeway system becomes competitive not cooperative, other implicatures are created and a distressful cycle is begun. Figure 1 indicates the stages of this cycle.

Figure 1

Normal Driving State: Tacit Expectation of Cooperation

VIOLATION OF EXPECTATION

Implicature

INTERPRETATION of Hostility or Incompetence

Consequence One: Personal Upset

Possible Consequence: Non-cooperative Action

The Cooperative Principle of Freeway Driving

One explanation of why the freeway tends to multiply competitive and hostile behavior is that communication is severely reduced, especially the kind of communication that would allow hostile implicatures to be reinterpreted. If during conversation I implicate that you are unworthy, you can always check my intentions. But on the freeway, the chances to reinterpret the implicatures rarely exist. According to Bliersbach and Dellen (1980), "Communicative coordination with other drivers is disturbed":

> Shut up in his 'tin box' with the communicative repertoire of a reduced "restricted code"... the driver is left alone with his assumptions and fears, which prove all the more negative the less he is able to control them through reality (481).

For example, if a driver pulls in front of me and violates the maxim <u>Be safe</u>, I automatically infer that he or she cares nothing for my survival. Not only is the other driver unable to make his genuine intentions known, but during freeway driving, curiously, good intentions do not matter. Even if I were to discover that the other driver does not want to hurt me but is only incompetent, I might be equally as angry. Incompetent drivers, I might think, should not be driving. The fact is that once drivers inter the freeway system, they are expected to cooperate, and that means being safe and being swift.

The second major consequence of uncooperative driving—its effect on the system—is well documented by Thomas C. Shelling. His book <u>Micromotives and Macrobehavior</u> "explores the relation between the behavior characteristics of the individuals who comprise some social aggregate, and the characteristics of the aggregate" (1978). Since Shelling's work supports the validity of a cooperative principle of driving, it will be reviewed carefully.

Shelling's interest is in those cases, including freeway driving, where people:

> Are responding to each other's behavior and influencing each other's behavior. People are responding to an environment that consists of people responding to an environment of people responses. Sometimes their dynamics are sequential; if your lights induce me to turn mine on, mine may induce somebody else but not you. Sometimes the dynamics are reciprocal; hearing your car horn, I honk mine, thus encouraging you to honk more insistently (14).

Schelling stresses the fact that people in cooperative systems like freeway driving are both individuals and part of the system. Contrary to most descriptions of driving, his examples contain individual people with their own preferences and goals, people who act "purposively." Yet in seeking these goals their behavior is constrained by the environment that consists of other people who are also pursuing their goals "What we typically have," he says, "is a mode of <u>contingent behavior</u>—behavior that depends on what others are doing" (17). For example, he states, "How you drive depends on how others drive; where you park depends on where others park…If your problem is that there is too much traffic, you are part of the problem" (27).

Perhaps Schelling's key argument for this discussion is that a driver can be part of the problem even when trying to be part of the solution. He describes this social interdependence in an extended anecdote entitled "The Social Contract." It is worth quoting here because it shows how the frustration of drivers is increased and perpetuated by other drivers.

The Cooperative Principle of Freeway Driving

A strange phenomenon on Boston's Southeast Expressway is reported by the traffic helicopter. If a freak accident, or a severe one, occurs in the southbound lane in the morning, it slows the northbound rush-hour traffic more than on the side where the obstruction occurs. People slow does to enjoy a look at the wreckage on the other side of the divider. Curiosity has the same effect as a bottleneck. Even the driver who, when he arrives at the site, is ten minutes behind schedule is likely to feel that ht's paid the price of admission and, though the highway is at least clear in front of him, will not resume speed until he's had his look, too.

Eventually large numbers of commuters have spent an extra ten minutes driving for a ten-second look. (Ironically, the wreckage may have been cleared away, but they spend their ten seconds looking for it, induced by the people ahead of them who seemed to be looking at something.) What kind of bargain is it? A few of them, offered a speedy bypass, might have stayed in line out of curiosity; most of them, after years of driving, know that when they get there what they're like to see is worth about ten seconds' driving time. When they get to the scene, the ten minutes delay is a sunk cost; their own sightseeing costs them only the ten seconds. It also costs ten seconds a piece to the tree score motorists crawling along behind them.

Everybody pays his ten minutes and gets his look But he pays ten seconds for his own look and nine minutes, fifty seconds for the curiosity of the drivers ahead of them. It is a bad bargain (125).

Schelling's work provides background evidence to the cooperative model of driving. Contrary to many solitary models of driving, the freeway drivers cannot ever <u>drive alone</u>; they are part of an elaborate system whose participants demand a great deal of cooperation from each other in order to make it run smoothly.

The explanatory power of the cooperative model does not end here, however. In the next sections the model will be tested against the existing behavioral and psycho-social models.

Testing the Cooperative Principle: The Cooperative Model vs. the Behaviorist Model

The Cooperative Model of driving is the antithesis to the behavioral model. Rather than posit an organism that reacts to the stimuli of the roadway, the Cooperative Model posits an interpreting human engaged in a rational activity. Most importantly, the two models are opposed in the way they account for learning to drive. Ray Fuller's model of driving as "threat avoidance," for example, states that the driver becomes more experienced—and thus safer—through a variety of positive and negative experiences that show him how to avoid threats to his safety. However, the negative experiences—or near accident—are the most significant for Fuller. Yet Fuller imagines that as important as these negative experiences are, they will not occur frequently enough for drivers on "forgiving road systems." He states:

> The learning of the consequences of one's actions in particular stimulus situations is clearly fundamental to the learning of safe driving. This includes the experience of both positive and negative consequences although the latter may be somewhat attenuated by the 'forgiving' nature of many road systems,

particularly where the error of one driver is corrected or compensated by the actions of another or others (1984:1146).

Fuller states that a cooperative or "forgiving" road system actually "attenuates" or lessens the kind of negative learning experiences that are crucial to becoming an experienced driver.

Fuller's quote brings up two important points. The first is that even scholarly attempts to posit a solitary competitive model of driving often contain evidence that points the opposite way—toward driving systems that are cooperative. The second point is Fuller's model seems unconcerned with the mental health and physical stress of drivers. While Fuller makes the primary learning experience of driving a near accident or a moment of danger, those experiences bring the driver a great deal of stress. A 1978 UC Irvine study of 100 drivers showed driving stress was directly related to the number of times a motorist need to apply his brakes in traffic (Seale 986:115).

The cooperative model has several advantages over the behavioral one. First, it does not require negative and stressful experiences. Second, it would not dismiss the importance of 'forgiving' road systems, as Fuller does, but explains what makes that system forgiving and try to teach those practices in traffic safety programs.

The Cooperative Principle and the Psycho-Social Model

Bliersbach and Dellen's ground-breaking 1980 study in German traffic psychology tried to account for the psycho-social dimensions of driving that other studies ignored. They were particularly interested in how drivers felt toward one another on the roadway, and where these feelings came from. Their original goal was to challenge the simplistic slogans of the German Safety council that say drivers should develop a "Partnership" with one another on the roadway. They conclude that "We will only discover the other driver as a partner if we have first of all discovered ourselves as drivers" (486).

Bliersbach and Dellen provide significant evidence that driving is not merely a technical matter. They show that, on the contrary, drivers are complete human beings who interact with other drivers and that driving is a complete psycho-social activity. Nevertheless, their conclusions are disappointing because of the weight they place on the "conflicts" between drivers. In fact, they argue for an essentially non-cooperative model of driving (484). However, even though their data is chosen to support their competitive model, by reinterpreting this data through the cooperative model, a significant cooperative dimension of driving emerges. Moreover, the cooperative model provides an explanation for the competitiveness that drivers feel that their study does not attempt.

> Let us begin by examining two of their archetypal driving scenarios. A very archetypal motorway situation with a completely everyday interaction can be cited. A driver who is in the process of overtaking (or beginning to overtake) notices in his rear-view mirror a driver approaching, flashing his lights and signaling that he wishes to fine the overtaking lane empty. The majority of drivers experience such an unreasonable demand as an outrageous insult from the injustice that their right to overtake is being challenged. In addition there is their rage at being at the mercy of the flashing driver bearing down from behind. Important in this is that the majority of motorists react with revenge techniques that result in hardening and escalation of this interaction. For the man behind will now unleash his anger all the more strongly

(its justification having just been confirmed by the man in front) by driving close behind—the striking demonstration of the common anger at the mutual obstruction (482).

Bliersbach and Dellen demonstrate the "common anger at the mutual obstruction" these drivers feel, yet they do not explain why this anger occurs. They provide no theory for understanding why this particular scenario causes such frustration.

Let us now reinterpret this anecdote through the cooperative model. In this anecdote, the slowest driver violates the maxim <u>Be Swift</u>, frustrating the driver who wants to pass. But the third driver, who pulls up closely behind the second driver, forcing him to pass before being ready, violates the maxim <u>Be Safe</u>. The second driver is frustrated on two counts: his expectations of cooperation have been violated by both drivers; both maxims are violate at once. It is, therefore, no surprise that drivers recount this kind of scenario as classically frustrating, competitive, and insulting.

A second anecdote that is central to a theory of competitive driving involves motorists who plan to drive at a leisurely pace, say for sightseeing, but are "forced to cooperate" by other drivers and must speed up to match the traffic flow. Drivers who have been "forced" this way usually explain that they feel pressured to go faster because "they were afraid that other drivers would regard them as incompetent" (482). In addition, these drivers generalized that the "experience of feeling obliged to do something: is the worst part of the driving.

On the surface, Bliersbach and Dellen's study seems to justify a truly conflicting model of driving; the subjects of the study not only expected cooperation, they actually felt insulted, threatened and "forced to cooperate" over their wishes.

Nevertheless, without discounting the legitimacy of the drivers' feelings, an alternative explanation can be presented.

According to the cooperative principle, the pressure that drivers feel to speed up or cooperate does not come from other drivers, per se. It is not that some drivers are inherently hostile. The pressure actually comes from the unwritten rules of the system in which all drivers who take the highway take part. In the above cases, drivers were forced to either speed up or slow down in order to coordinate their speed with other drivers. Since demands make them feel that there is absolutely no cooperation to be expected on the highway. In fact, feeling "pressured to cooperate" implies that one can, on some occasions, not cooperate while driving. That is not the case. Every driver unconsciously expects cooperation; the frustration arises when this expectation is violated.

The Cooperative Model: Rules Over Laws

The cooperative principle of freeway driving posits that the only "rule of the road" is "Make your contribution as required at the state at which it occurs" and that all other rules are merely variations of the basic expectation of cooperation. However, since such an idea is counter-intuitive, we must investigate the matter further. Does the cooperative principle—as the essential rule of freeway driving—make formal rules and laws meaningless or even counterproductive? There is good evidence that this may be the case. Taylor (1976) argues that models of driving that try to establish strict laws or formal rules of proper driving will always be insufficient. What is important is not the rules that make driving work, he says, but the ways that different rule systems interact in the driving task and the ways that drivers choose to interpret these. Driving is not a formal rule system but an interaction of various rule systems all of which deserve investigation (Taylor, 1976, 1980). Citing

Hargreaves' distinctions between normative, implemental, probabilistic, and interpretive types of rule systems (Hargreaves 1980), Taylor argues that a proper description of human driving must account for how and why all of these different kinds of rules apply.

Schelling also argues that laws do not account for the most important behavior of people. As he says, "People's behavior depends on how many are behaving a particular way or how much they are behaving that way" (94). The fact is, laws are useless unless people decide to comply with them, and if people do comply, they do so for better reasons than merely following laws. Schelling writes:

> A social planner can usefully contemplate traffic signals. They remind us that, though planning is often associated with control, the crucial element is often coordination. People need to do the right things at the right time in relation to what others are doing (121).

As Schelling emphasizes it is coordination, not control that counts.

The cooperative model of driving cannot be reduced to formal rules or traffic laws that would dictate to drivers what they should do. The rules of cooperative driving are "aleatory" rules in that they are rules that change as the activity occurs. For instance, being cooperative might require going faster in some cases or hitting the brakes in another.

The Limits of Laws

The kinds of rules that the cooperative principle provides cannot be reduced to formal rules or traffic laws. In fact, there is evidence that some laws actually impede the proper functioning of the cooperative principle. For example, a recent campaign by Caltrans has tried to eliminate the notion of the "right of way" and replace it with the idea of "privilege of way." The reason for this campaign is the discovery by traffic engineers that the notion of the "right of way" actually creates problems because people take what they think is their right even though the consequences are uncooperative. The idea of the "right of way" allows people to justify their unfair or uncooperative behavior by an appeal to what seems like a natural right.

What <u>Try Highway Navigation</u> tries to do is explain exactly what the term "right of way" means. An example of their discussion follows:

> When two cars approach an intersection at the same time, who has the right of way? Did you say, "The car on the right?" That's wrong! Under the California Vehicle code, no one ever has the right of way. Someone is required to yield the right of way… to give another driver the privilege of going first. Failing to yield the right of way is a violation of our traffic laws. We're talking about more than just a play on words… Right of way is a talking expression that can easily provoke an argument and the combat weapons are two tons of steel on wheels.
>
> In California, we want drivers to get along with each other so we yield to them. We give the other driver the privilege of using the road and then we have the freedom to go…

In several places, the safety course makes the following point— that courtesy and cooperation are more important than rules or rights:

The Cooperative Principle of Freeway Driving

When four cars stop at a four-way stop intersection, who must yield the right of way? We have no California law to cover this situation.

So, someone has to be courteous and wave to the driver on his right indicating that he should go first. Then, the right of way laws will work for the other drivers (16).

This example is significant because it reverses the hierarchy that most people assume. Instead of laws creating fairness and cooperation, it is actually courtesy that allows the law to work. Secondly, the example supports Schelling's point that driving behavior is often influenced less by laws than by what others do. Finally, it supports the point of this thesis—that traffic safety campaigns should emphasize the underlying cooperative principle at work when driving.

Laws of driving allow people to feel separate from the cooperative system that makes traffic work and to avoid social responsibility—that is the argument of an interesting study by Bruce F. Herms, "Pedestrian Crosswalk Study: Accidents in Painted and Unpainted Crosswalks." Herms discovers that approximately twice as many pedestrian accidents occur in marked (or painted) crosswalks as in unmarked crosswalks. The reason for this anomaly is that a "reflection on the pedestrians' attitude and lack of caution when using the marked crosswalk" (11).

Yet this phenomenon is also understandable through the cooperative principle: My hypothesis is that pedestrians in marked crosswalks feel legally separated from the traffic system and thus free not to cooperate. As jaywalking tickets make clear, pedestrians have a tendency to forget their interconnectedness with drivers. The painted crosswalk, like a law, or the "right of way," makes people believe they are not part of the system. They believe the painted crosswalk will protect them. On the other hand, when crosswalks are not painted, pedestrians separate themselves from the traffic flow; they must pay attention to how their actions influence the actions of other drivers. They must make their contribution to the exchange at the state at which it is required.

That laws often restrain driving instead of coordinating it is also argued by Charles Lave, in "Speeding, Coordination, and the 55 MPH Limit":

> For peculiar historical reasons, speed laws evolved as <u>limits</u> on driver behavior, rather than as signaling devices meant to <u>coordinate</u> it. Guided by the limit-rationale, police concentrate on those drivers who exceed the legal speed, and tend to ignore those drivers who disrupt coordination by traveling much slower than the norm (1159).

Contrary to the behaviorist model, Lave argues that there is no statistically discernible relationship between the fatality rate and average speed. He demonstrates that it is "Variance kills, not speed." In other words, when most cars are traveling at nearly the same speed, whether that speed is high or low, the fatality rate will be low. Lave's practical recommendation is that traffic officers should change their priority. They should concentrate on arresting the drivers whose speed is at great variance from others, not merely the fast drivers. They should do this, "because slow drivers are as much a public hazard as fast ones" (1163).

While Lave's evidence is compelling, his recommendation is rather simplistic because he has no explicit model of driving to support his generalizations. Restated in the terms of the cooperative principle, Lave's argument would be this: police should change their focus; instead of concentrating on arresting drivers who drive <u>fast</u>, they should concentrate on those who violate the norm or standard, whether they go too fast or too slow. In other words, traffic safety campaigns should concentrate on drivers who violate the cooperative principle of the roadway.

The Implicature of BABY ON BOARD

The cooperative principle asserts that underlying the competitiveness that most drivers feel is an implicit cooperative system. Perhaps the best way to support this assumption is to explain in cooperative terms a phenomenon that most people experience as competitive and hostile. The phenomenon I've chosen is one known to nearly everyone" the present controversy over and reaction to the "Baby on Board" warning signs that drivers place in their rear window.

According to a recent article in the <u>Los Angeles Times</u> (March 2, 1986) entitled " 'Baby on Board' Signs Kick Up a Fuss: Criticized by Safety Officials, They Also Inspire Sardonic Parodies by Offended Motorists," the signs "Baby on Board" or "Child in Car" have created quite a harsh reaction. Part of this angry reaction can be seen in the alternative signs that have been purchased or produced that say things like "Beagle on Board," "Lover on Board," and more caustic ones like "Baby in Trunk." In addition, a controversy rages among safety experts, who feel that the signs are not only hazardous but selfish. Stephanie Tonbrello, executive director of the Inglewood-based Child Passenger Safety Association, states that "I've seen the signs stuck in the middle of the back window, where they might prevent you from seeing a kid walking behind the car." She adds, "You have to protect everyone's kid, not just your own."

Why has this controversy arisen? Are Americans merely non-sentimental about children? That seems unlikely, since commercials and advertising remind us that we are in a second baby boom. Are

Americans merely mean-spirited? That also seems unlikely. The best explanation may come from the cooperative principle.

As the cooperative principle states, all drivers expect others to <u>Be Safe</u>. Yet signs like "Child in Car" ask for special caution; they make explicit what everyone knows. As Grice would say, these signs violate the maxim of Quantity—"Do not give more information than is necessary." The implicature of the baby signs, then, is two fold: 1) They imply that you are not acting as cautiously as you can anyway, and 2) They imply that the driver with a child deserves special cautions that other drivers, including yourself, do not.

In this example, as in the previous ones, the cooperative principle not only accounts for driving phenomena but actually explains that phenomena in more depth.

Chapter IV

Results and Discussion

Results

In testing the explanatory power of the cooperative model of driving against the data from existing traffic studies and from phenomenon that most drivers are familiar with everyday, the following results can be seen:

1) The cooperative principle exposes the limitations of the behavioral model of driving while highlighting evidence of cooperation and "forgiving road systems" that the behavioral model excludes form consideration.
2) The cooperative principle provides a significant reinterpretation of psycho-social models that demonstrate the competitiveness and frustration of driving by identifying these frustrations as breakdowns in the underlying cooperative system.
3) The cooperative principle provides a way of understanding the freeway as a rule-based system that cannot be codified into strict laws by law officers and actually exposes the limitations of many freeway driving laws.
4) The cooperative principle offers a complete and rather complex analysis of the recent controversy over the "Baby on Board" signs.

Discussion

Perhaps the most significant aspect of this study is that it poses a direct challenge to the idea that the freeway must be a solitary, competitive, and hostile environment. Such an attitude is not an illusion: most drivers share that perception. Further, such an idea is promoted and perpetuated in popular advertising and is the dominant model among traffic specialists.

This study also emphasizes that most accounts of the freeway experience limit themselves by not considering the psycho-social reality in which drivers find themselves, a reality in which driving can be seen as expressive not instrumental, cooperative not competitive, and systematic not chaotic.

Nevertheless, to complete the study merely by demonstrating the superiority of the cooperative model to explain driving phenomena would be irresponsible to two professions: the first would be that of traffic psychology, which is essentially an applied psychology field and tries to make the driving system more efficient and safe; the second would be the field of psychotherapy, my chosen field, which is dedicated to understanding human beings to improve their mental health and their practical success.

Because of this practical demand for my study, I must now move from theory to practice and make specific recommendations for improving the freeway system and the mental health of Los Angeles drivers.

Chapter V

Recommendations

From Theory to Practice

At the conclusion of their study that brought psycho-social dimensions into traffic theories, Bleirsbach and Dellen conclude with the need for traffic safety programs to consider their findings. They state:

> It would be important for a traffic educational programme to work out the patterns of driving as well as the involved interaction conflicts meticulously and didactically. Therefore, the existing lack of language concerning the processes of driving must be remedied. Essential to traffic education is a language by which the psycho-social processes of driving could be communicated and which at the same time would give drivers an instrument for identifying their own patterns of driving—and for realizing the interaction effects which are caused by their driving patterns (486).

In what follows, I would like to develop a "language by which the psycho-social processes of driving could be communicated." That language would have one message: bad driving is done by drivers who do not realize their interdependence on the driving system and on other drivers.

I believe that this model for educating drivers can have significant impact in two domains: the first would be traffic safety campaigns and traffic violators' schools, whose goal is to make driving more efficient, reduce congestions, and to reduce the stress that accompanies freeway driving. The second domain would be psychotherapy, whose goal would be to view the freeway as a place where patients manifest their psycho-social behavior in a concentrated way.

Traffic Safety Campaigns

The primary means by which traffic safety is promulgated among drivers is by traffic safety propaganda. Based on the behaviorist model of driving, this literature is designed to provide vicarious negative experiences for drivers by pointing out the consequences of their unsafe behavior. The following is a sample list of slogans that appear in this literature:

> Be smart—Stay 4 Seconds Apart
> Visibility Low? Go Slow!
> Parking Double Invites Trouble!
> Reduce Speed at Night to the Distance of Sight
> Kids Move Fast! Drive Slow!
> Every Near Accident is a Warning!
> Expect Pedestrians to Do the Unexpected!
> April Showers Bring Reduced Visibility and
> Increased Stopping Distance
> Watch the Other Guy As Well As the Signal
> Distractions Can Cause Accidents (National Safety Council, 1986).

On traffic safety posters, these slogans are usually accompanied by cartoons that show the consequences of not obeying the slogans

(See Appendix 1). According to the behavioral model, each poster is supposed to function like a vicarious "near accident," an experience that motivates safer driving.

A pamphlet produced by the National Safety Council entitled "Get It On!" illustrates the influence of the mechanistic and behavioral models on existing safety campaigns. The cover of the pamphlet reveals only half of what appears to be the face of a pretty young woman. When the right side of the cover is opened, the other side of the woman's face—bruised and bandaged—is revealed, along with a message "Safety Belts Do Make a Difference: Get it Together!" The next prose has the title "Public Apathy—HIGHWAY KILLER" and the statistical possibility of being injured in a car accident:

During a Typical 75-Years Lifespan You:
*Will Experience a Traffic Crash
*Have a 50% Chance of Suffering
*Have One Chance in 50 of Becoming a Fatality

Effectiveness of 70% Safety Belt Usage
*9,140 Lives Save Each Year
*327,000 Injuries Reduced or Prevented Annually

The weakness of such an approach to modify driver behavior is already pointed out by Taylor (1981), whose studies show that "People will not in general believe in the statistical association between their actions and accidents, unless it is part of their experience" (491). Thus, such an approach seems destined to fail. However, not all safety pamphlets reveal these weaknesses.

A pamphlet entitled "The Designated Driver: Being a Friend" incorporates the psycho-social dimensions of driving and asserts the interdependence of drivers. The program is to keep drivers from driving drunk.

> The principle behind the program is simple. One individual volunteers to refrain from drinking alcoholic beverages, thereby assuring the safe transportation home of the remaining guests in the group. (National Safety Council, 1986).

The proposal considers a mutual enterprise among drivers and friends, rather than a competition; moreover, it emphasizes the positive consequences of one driver taking the time to be courteous, such as Schelling (1978) suggests.

In general, traffic safety literature is designed primarily to avoid accidents and arrest; it does not try to promote cooperative driving or efficient freeway driving. If the cooperative principle of driving were promoted through safety propaganda, it would have to remind drivers of the underlying the cooperative system and the significance of violations. It would try to convince them that their competitive attitude gets in the way of smooth and efficient freeway use.

Traffic Violators' Schools

The second means by which the state educates drivers is through traffic violators' schools. The goal of the traffic violators' schools, at least according to Russ Furnas, traffic officer, is to change the notion of a ticket from a punishment to a preventative measure. He says that by educating millions of people to use their seat belts and drive defensively, the amount of accidents will become reduced to a predictable level.

Furnas believes that traffic school works where other methods fail because it places drivers in a "legally compromising position," where they are ready to hear safety messages.

The methods of traffic schools vary a great deal; some use primarily "scare tactics" like filmstrips; others use a rational approach and spend most time in discussion. Some use reading and writing; others only talking. Still, despite the surface differences, there remains a common underlying practice in all traffic schools. For instance, in all schools, the instructor is the primary force of authority in the room. Second, the primary approach to prevent accidents and tickets is through slogans, statistics, and rules of thumb: for example, "Seventy-three percent of all accidents occur in intersections," "If it's convenient, it's probably illegal," and so on.

However, sometimes the traffic officer will allow his own perceptions to come out, and it is often then that true education goes on. Interestingly, these moments usually expand the importance of driving and consider its psycho-social dimensions. For example, according to Russ Furnas, there is a direct relationship between a driver's personality and driving record. He says that "traffic citations are a statement about where you are in your life," and "if you violate a valid law, there must be something wrong with you." These statements are merely based on intuition; they are not supported by studies; however, we can assume that the intuition of a traffic officer suggests the need for more studies in this area. It also suggests that traffic officers are willing to impart psycho-social aspects of driving; they only need the proper information.

Even when traffic school instructors have a great deal of intuitive insight about how driving and life relate, the structure of the traffic school does not allow these connections to be discussed. In the traffic schools I have studied, there is very little communication between the drivers during the sessions. Participants look and act as if they have lost their self-worth; they look like bad students who have come to be lectured at for eight hours. Within this structure, where the cooperative and collaborative dimensions of learning are absent, it is unlikely that the cooperative aspects of driving can be realized. Fortunately, however, alternative models of traffic school are being considered.

Alfred W. Clark and Robert J. Powell (1984) discuss an alternative model of traffic education in their article, "Changing Drivers' Attitudes Through Peer Group Decision." In earlier studies (Clark 1976) it was demonstrated that "peers emerged as critical role senders, either reinforcing or opposing official prescriptions about respect for the law…." For the most recent study, peer group members were selected, and group discussions were held about various aspects of driving, some of which include the following:

> What do you think about the notion that a person should be able to drive at any speed they think is safe? Is there any such thing as courtesy on the road? What do you think about the way other people drive? Do you often find yourself in a situation where you get frustrated on the road? What do you do in such a situation? What do you think is the attitude of the police toward young drivers….(158).

One notices immediately that these questions implicitly support the cooperative model because they ask individual drivers to see themselves as part of the larger system. Even Clark and Powell realize that the study is unique:

> This is a radical departure from the traditional fear-arousal approach, still characteristic of most safety campaigns around the world. Both the emergent U.S. approach and

the present study avoid aversive conditioning and focus on the reinforcement of desired attitudes and behavior provided by the approval of peer groups (cf. Skinner, 1975) (161).

Besides being radical, the results proved quite positive. According to pre-tests and post-tests, the groups who engaged in discussions showed significant change in attitude toward driving compared to similar test groups that did not hold discussions.

Is the study replicable? The cooperative principle suggests that it is, even though the terms of the study must be changed. While this study is based on the behavioral model—trying to use peer group leaders to influence driving—the same practice can be followed without the behavioral paradigm. For example, the questions that opened the discussions would cause rational discussion among all drivers, not only those of the same peer group. One might say that when it comes to driving, all drivers are peers. If that is so, "peer leaders" could be influential in other discussion groups as well. Even without the behavioral model, the discussion process would emphasize the shared experiences of drivers, thus reducing alienation and competitiveness. If run correctly, it could have the same effect as group therapy, allowing each driver to express his or her individual frustrations about the driving system and receiving feedback from others. Such a method has already proved successful with rape victims, Vietnam veterans, alcoholics, drug addicts, abused children, and others.

The potential success of "freeway rap groups" is also suggested by Taylor's hermeneutic model of driving (Taylor 1981). Since driving is an interpretive activity, Taylor states, proper driving, whether safe or efficient, can be learned through discussion:

Assuming that safe behavior is not innate, and that it should not be acquired only by direct experience (i.e. accidents), some persuasive process must take place. The scientific paradigm emphasizes the acquisition of skills and knowledge of contingencies; the hermeneutical paradigm is more concerned with how to interpret and evaluate situations, and how certain actions are regarded by people in the culture (493).

What Taylor considers the most important lesson to be learned—"How certain actions are regarded by people in the culture"—can only be learned if traffic schools are designed so that peers can discuss their relation to the freeway system.

Therapy and Driving

Just as a proper traffic violators' school would have aspects of group therapy, therapy sessions can also benefit from some of the results of this study. I would like to close this study by making specific recommendations to this end.

As the cooperative model asserts, the violations of cooperation on the freeway require an interpretation. While we notice the implicature immediately, and while the danger of that implicature may cause us a physical reaction, the most important part of the process is how we interpret the violation.

In many cases, our interpretations of implicatures are based on our past experience. A conversational implicature will serve as an example. Let us say that you are in the kitchen and I summon you. If you do not respond in less than three-tenths of a second, an implicature occurs. Either you did not hear me, or you are ignoring me, you have left the room, and so on. Numerous interpretations are possible for the one implicature. Normally, the least dramatic are preferred. But not always. Sometimes the failed response to a summons can recreate very deep feelings, feelings of being ignored or abandoned that arise from childhood experiences. Implications allow for interpretations, and interpretations bring in our total experience, including our subconscious experiences.

Implicatures on the freeway can have the same consequence. Somewhere between the strictly physical response to stressful incidents on the freeway and the general frustration that most people express lies a range of feelings unique to that individual driver. Why, for instance, do some people pursue conflicts on the freeway for several miles? Why do some return hostile gestures and others not? Why do some continue the fight outside of their cars?

One example of how deeply freeway implicatures affect us can be seen in the ways that bad driving behavior in others brings out racist and sexist hostility. A phenomenon that is familiar to almost everyone is a driver referring angrily to another driver by labeling their sex, race, or class. Why does this happen?

One explanation, which points toward the strength of the cooperative principle, is this: freeway driving tends to make all drivers equal in the system; cooperation is required of them all, regardless of their individual characteristics or the value of their automobile. That is to say, that the freeway system is actually a great leveler. It does not matter who you are, what you are driving, where you have been, or where you are going. Yet this democratization is the antithesis to the motives of many drivers who select their vehicles to distinguish themselves from others. When the shared cooperative system becomes apparent—which it does <u>only when it is</u> <u>violated</u>—the frustration is multiplied by the feeling of anonymity. The anger and frustration manifests itself in a need to increase self-esteem, which causes the angered driver to distinguish him or herself from the driver who violated the cooperative principle. One way to do this is with socio-economic labeling.

Again, although such a hypothesis requires a great deal more testing, the link between driving and self-esteem cannot be underestimated.

The Viscott Method and Freeways

Another reason that psychotherapists can benefit from understanding the cooperative principle is demonstrated by David Viscott in his book Risking. To illustrate the need for risking and commitment in everyday life, Viscott uses the example of driving:

> Passing in an automobile illustrates the dangers involved in taking other risks. Passing is the most dangerous moment in driving, when most fatalities occur. The driver most likely to be killed is the one who hesitates, loses his nerve and can neither accelerate nor apply his brakes. He cannot follow through on a commitment to act (56).

He goes on to say, "The passing situation is largely the creation of each driver. In it he finds the conflicts, the ambivalence and the lack of resolve that attend his actions in everyday life" (71). If it is true that as Viscott says, "All risking follows the model of passing," it could be equally true that all risking follows the model of other risky experiences on the freeway, such as merging into the flow of traffic at the gore point, as we discussed in Chapter 2. The connections between how human beings react to others on the freeway and how they react to them outside of their automobiles has yet to be fully explored, and psychotherapists should be interested in studying this matter further.

Long-Range Consequences

The Cooperative Principle and the Synergistic Society

What might happen if all the people who saw driving as a competitive, even war-like, task began to see it as a cooperative system where responsibility and commitment are required? The end result could be a partial transformation of society, a possibility partially explored by Frank G. Goble in <u>The Third Force</u>: <u>The Psychology of Abraham Maslow</u>.

Goble relates the research by Ruth Benedict into the difference between societies of "high synergy" and "low synergy." The high synergy societies were those that cooperated together for the mutual advantage of all, not because they were unselfish, but because custom had established ways that cooperation was made worthwhile. Benedict says,

> Societies where non-aggression is conspicuous, have social orders in which the individual, by the same act and at the same time, serves his own advantage and that of the group… Non-aggression occurs, not because people are unselfish and put social obligations above personal desires, but when social arrangements make these two identical (in Goble 108).

Bad or non-synergic societies are those "where the advantage of one individual becomes a victory over another, and the majority who are not victorious must shift as they can" (in Goble 109).

This non-synergistic society sounds very similar to the driving system that is posited by Bliersbach and Dellen (1980) where drivers come to "expect no cooperation from other drivers" and drive "literally alone" (484). While the cooperative principle challenges this statement (because no one can be "literally" alone), it is true that one can be "socially alone," alienated, angered, frightened. What is needed instead is an arrangement where individuals engaged in a mutually rational and beneficial activity like freeway driving can act in a way that one person's advantage is another's advantage. As Schelling writes:

> People do things, or abstain from doing things, that affect others, beneficially or adversely. Without appropriate organization, the results may be pretty unsatisfactory. "Human nature" is easily blamed; but accepting that most people are more concerned with their own affairs than with the affairs of others, and more aware of their own concerns than of the concerns of others, we may find human nature less pertinent than social organization…What we need in these circumstances is an enforceable social contract. I'll cooperate if you and everybody else will. I'm better off if we all cooperate that if we go our separate ways (129).

The first step in accomplishing this social contract, however, would be the realization that, as Benedict, Schelling and others have demonstrated, cooperation and synergy create a healthier and more efficient society for everyone.

Since I began my study with a driving anecdote, it seems appropriate to close with another one. However, this one is from Sydney J. Harris, Field Newspaper Syndicate, and is entitled <u>Road Test</u>. It expresses a desire for a cooperative road system that this study tried to account for in a scholarly way.

A friend was driving me to the airport, and I noticed his remarkable courtly attitude toward other drivers. "It's my own private form of therapy," he explained. "It's the best way I know to bolster my ego."

"How does that work?" I asked, thinking of my own not altogether saintly driving habits.

"Well," he said, "most drivers are so miserable to one another that when they come across someone who is not competing and gives them the right of way, they practically break their necks nodding and waving. The psychological reward is tremendous. I drive along feeling like a prince."

"Don't you ever get taken advantage of that way?" I inquired.

"That's the surprising thing," he said. "My courtesy makes other drivers more courteous. They suddenly seem to realize that they're behaving behind the wheel as they never would in any face-to-face situation."

"If every motorist acted as you did, "I observed, "then most of your pleasure would evaporate, because you'd be just another ordinary driver."

"When that great day comes," he said with a smile, "we'll all be so good that we won't need to get pleasure from being good. But don't idle your motor until then, my friend."

List of Resources

A.A.T.B.S. FAMILY THERAPY. 1982.

Andersson, A., Nilsson, A., and Hendricksson, N.G. Personality Differences Between Accident-Loaded and Accident-Free Young Car Drivers, British Journal of Psychology, 1970, 61:409-421.

Balter, M. Road Warriors. Los Angeles Times Magazine, February 2, 1986.

Bliersbach, G. and Dellen, R.G. Interaction Conflicts and Interaction Patterns in Traffic Situations. International Review of Applied Psychology, 1980, 29:475-489.

Bolton, R. Machismo in Motion: The Ethos of Peruvian Truckers. University Review of London, 1979, 7:312-342.

Brenner, B. and Selzer, M. Risk of Causing a Fatal Accident Associated With Alcoholism, Psychopathology and Stress: Further Analysis of Previous Data. Behavioral Science, 1969, 14:492-495.

California Department of Motor Vehicles. Try Highway Navigation: A Traffic Safety Course. 1984.

California Department of Motor Vehicles. 1984 Traffic Volumes. Sacramento, 1984.

Campbell, D. Reforms as Experiments. American Psychologist, 1969, 24:409-429.

Carlson, W.L. and Klein, D. Familial vs. Institutional Socialization of Young Traffic Offenders, Journal of Safety Research, 1970, 2:13-25.

Clark, A.W. A Social role Approach to Driver Behaviour. Perceptual and Motor Skills, 1976, 42:325-326.

Clark, A.W. and Powell, R. Changing Drivers' Attitudes Through Peer Group Decision. Human Relations, 1984, 37:155-162.

Cohen, John. BEHAVIOUR IN UNCERTAINTY. London: George Allen & Unwin Ltd., 1964.

Crancer, A. and Quiring, D. DRIVING RECORDS OF PERSONS HOSPITALIZED FOR SUICIDE GESTURES. Olympia: State of Washington Department of Motor Vehicles, 1968.

Crancer, A. and Quiring, D. The Chronic Alcoholic as Motor Vehicle Operator. Northwest Medicine, 1969a, 68:42-47.

Crancer, A. and Quiring, D. the Mentally Ill as Motor Vehicle Operator. American Journal Psychiatry, 1969b, 126:807-813.

Dow, D. The Heart of the Matter. KCBS, February 27, 1986.

Eelkema, R., Brosseau, J., Koshnick, R., and McGee, C. A Statistical Study on the Relationship Between Mental Illness and Traffic Accidents: A Pilot Study. American Journal of Public Health, 1970, 60:459-469.

Erhard, Werner. Definition of Upset. Erhard Seminar Training. 1981.

Foutz, L. OLYMPIC IMPACT REPORT. Los Angeles: Southern California Association of Governments, 1985.

Fuller, Ray. A Conceptualization of Driving Behaviour as Threat Avoidance. Ergonomics, 1984, 27:1139-1155.

Goble, Frank G. THE THIRD FORCE: THE PSYCHOLOGY OF ABRAHAM MASLOW. New York: Grossman, 1970.

Goffman, Erving. INTERACTION RITUAL: ESSAYS ON FACE-TO-FACE BEHAVIOR. New York: Penguin, 1967.

Goulding, A.P. Differential Accident Involvement: A Literature Survey. Council for Scientific and Industrial Research Reports, 1983.

Grice, H.P. Logic and Conversation. William James Lectures, Harvard, 1967.

Harvey, Steve. 'Baby on Board' Signs Kick Up a Fuss. Los Angeles Times, March 2, 1986.

Hargraves, D.H. Common Sense Models. MODELS OF MAN. (A.J. Chapman and D.M. Jones, eds.). Leicester: British Psychological Society, 1980, 215-225.

Herms, B. Pedestrian Crosswalk Study: Accidents in Painted and Unpainted Crosswalks. San Diego, CA: Public Works Department, Traffic Engineering Section, 1970.

Hutchinson, John W. and Roberts, John. Expressive Constraints on Driver Re-Education. PSYCHOLOGICAL ASPECTS OF DRIVER BEHAVIOR. Voorburg, The Netherlands: Institute for Road Safety Research, 1980.

Kennedy, P., Phanjoo, A., Shekim, W.O. Risk-taking in the Lives of Parasuicides (Attempted Suicides). British Journal of Psychiatry, 1971, 119:281-286.

Kincaid, James. New York Down, Washington Up. Commentary, 1986, 81:37.

Klein, James. The Teenage Driver: A Research Paradigm, Traffic Quarterly, 22, 97-108.

Klein, D. Adolescent Driving as Deviant Behavior. Journal of Safety Research, 1972, 4:98-105.

Lave, Charles A. Speeding, coordination, and the 55 MPH Limit. The American Economic Review, 1985, 75:1159-1163.

Levinson, Stephen (ed.). PRAGMATICS. Cambridge: Cambridge U Press, 1983.

Litman, R. and Tabachnick, N. Fatal One-Car Accidents. Psychoanalytic Quarterly, 1967, 36:248-249.

McGlade, F.S. ADJUSTMENTS BEHAVIOUR AND SAFE PERFORMANCE. Chicago, Illinois, Charles C. Thomas, 1970.

McKenna, F.P. The Human Factor in Driving Accidents: An Overview of Approaches and Problems. Ergonomics, 1982, 25:867-877.

McMurray, L. Emotional Stress and Driving Performance: The Effect of Divorce. Olympia: State of Washington Department of Motor Vehicle, 1968.

Mentzos, S. INTERPERSONAL AND INSTITUTIONAL RELATIONS. Frankfurt/Main: Suhrkamp, 1976.

Motor Vehicle Manufacturers Association. Get It On! Detroit, 1985.

Munjack, D. Personal Conversation, 1986.

Naatanen, R. and Summula, H. ROAD-USER BEHAVIOUR AND TRAFFIC ACCIDENTS. Amsterdam: North Holland, 1974.

National Safety Council. 1986 POSTER DIRECTORY. Chicago, 1986.

National Safety Council. The Designated Driver. Chicago, 1984.

Ortner, J. Freeway Management. Los Angeles: Automobile Club of Southern California, 1986.

Osman, M. A Psychoanalytic Study of Auto Accident Victims. Contemporary Psychoanalysis, 1968, $\underline{5}$:62-74.

Parsons, H.M. Caution Behavior and its Conditioning in Driving. Human Factors, 1976, $\underline{18}$:397-407.

Parsons, H.M. Behaviour Analysis in Highway Safety. Invited Address at the Annual Meeting of the Association for Behaviour Analysis, Dearborn, Michigan.

Perls, Fritz. THE GESTALT APPROACH & EYEWITNESS TO THERAPY. New York: Science and Behavior Books, 1973.

Risk, A. A Behavioural Theory of Driving and Accident Causation. In ROAD SAFETY: RESEARCH AND PRACTICE (Edited by H.C. Foot, A.J. Chapman and F.M. Wade) (Eastbourne: Praeger), 1981, 219-225.

Roberts, J.M., Hutchinson, J.W., and Hanscom, F.R. Traffic Control Decisions and Self-Testing Values: A Preliminary Study. Traffic Engineering, 1972, $\underline{42}$:12-28.

Roberts, J.M., Kozelka, R., and Arth, M. Some Highway Cultural Patterns, The Plains Anthropologist, 1956, 8:3-14.

Roper, D. The Heart of the Matter. KCBS. February 27, 1986.

Rugoff, R. The Freeway. California Living. April 13, 1986.

Schelling, Thomas C. MICROMOTIVES AND MACROBEHAVIOR. New York: Norton, 1978.

Schuman, S.H. Young Male Drivers: Impulse, Expression, Accidents and Violations. American Medical Association Journal, 1967, 200:1026-1030.

Schmidt, C., Perlin, S., Towns, W., Fisher, R. and Shaffer, J. Characteristics of Drivers Involved in Single-Car Accidents. Archives of General Psychiatry, 1972, 27:800-893.

Seale, J. Road Warriors. Los Angeles, January 1986.

Selzer, M. Fatal Traffic Accidents: The Turns to An Emergency Approach. University of Michigan Medical Center Journal, 1968, 34:102-105.

Shak, Clarence. The Transportation System of the Future, 1986

Shaw, L. and Sichel, H. ACCIDENT PRONENESS. Oxford: Pergamon, 1971.

Shotter, J. Men the Magicians: the Duality of Social Being and the Structure of Moral Worlds. In MODELS OF MAN (Edited by A.J. Chapman and D.M. Jones) (Leicester: British Psychological Society), 1980, 13-34.

Sporli, S. Verkehrpsychologie swischen Machen and Lieben. Gruppendynamik, 1978, 9:228-238.

Tabachnick, N., Gussen, J., Litman, R., Peck, M.L., Tiber, N., Wold, C.I. ACCIDENT OR SUICIDE: DESTRUCTION BY AUTOMOBILE. Springfield: Thomas, 1973.

Taylor, D.H. Accidents, Risks, Models of Explanation. Human Factors, 1976, 18:217-280.

Taylor, D.H. The New Psychology in Transport Research. PROCEEDINGS OF THE WORLD CONFERENCE ON TRANSPORT RESEARCH. London, 1980.

Taylor, D.H. The Hermeneutics of Accidents and Safety. Ergonomics, 1981, 24:487-495.

Thayer, C. The Heart of the Matter. KCBS. February, 27, 1986.

Turfboer, R. Do People Really Drive as They Live? Traffic Quarterly, 1967, 21:101-108.

Wilde, G.J.S. Social Interaction Patterns in Driver Behavior: An Introductory Review. Human Factors, 1976, 18:477-492.

Wilde, G.J.S. Objective And Subjective Risk in Drivers' Response to Road Conditions. Paper Presented to Seminar on the Implications of Risk Taking Theories for Traffic Safety. West Berlin, 1981.

Winch, P. THE IDEA OF SCIENCE AND ITS RELATIONS TO PHILOSOPHY. London: Routledge & Kegan Paul, 1958.

www.ingramcontent.com/pod-product-compliance
Lightning Source LLC
LaVergne TN
LVHW041536060526
838200LV00037B/1005